Mexican American Psychology

Mexican American Psychology

Social, Cultural, and Clinical Perspectives

Mario A. Tovar

Race, Ethnicity, Culture, and Health
Regan A. R. Gurung, Series Editor

 PRAEGER™

An Imprint of ABC-CLIO, LLC
Santa Barbara, California • Denver, Colorado

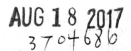
Library of Congress Cataloging-in-Publication Data

Names: Tovar, Mario A. (Mario Alberto)
Title: Mexican American psychology : social, cultural, and clinical
 perspectives / Mario A. Tovar.
Description: Santa Barbara, California : Praeger, an Imprint of ABC-CLIO,
 LLC, [2017] | Series: Race, ethnicity, culture, and health | Includes
 bibliographical references and index.
Identifiers: LCCN 2016057092 (print) | LCCN 2017002781 (ebook) | ISBN
 9781440841477 (hard copy : alk. paper) | ISBN 9781440841484 (e-book)
Subjects: LCSH: Mexican Americans—Psychology. | Mexican Americans—Social
 life and customs. | Mexican Americans—Health and hygiene. | Mexican
 Americans—Mental health.
Classification: LCC RC451.5.M48 T68 2017 (print) | LCC RC451.5.M48 (ebook) |
 DDC 362.2089/68073—dc23
LC record available at https://lccn.loc.gov/2016057092

ISBN: 978-1-4408-4147-7
EISBN: 978-1-4408-4148-4

21 20 19 18 17   1 2 3 4 5

This book is also available as an eBook.

Praeger
An Imprint of ABC-CLIO, LLC

ABC-CLIO, LLC
130 Cremona Drive, P.O. Box 1911
Santa Barbara, California 93116-1911
www.abc-clio.com

This book is printed on acid-free paper ∞

Manufactured in the United States of America

Contents

Series Foreword

There are clearly many different cultural approaches to health, and it is of great importance for health care workers, psychologists, and the administrations who support them to be culturally aware. Knowing about the different approaches to health can also help the lay consumer be better appraised of cultural differences which in turn can lead to a reduction in stereotyping or prejudicial attitudes toward behaviors that may be seen to be different from the norm. This volume represents the first in a series of titles, each designed to focus on a subgroup representing the diversity of America.

Each book in this series—Race, Ethnicity, Culture, and Health—provides a comprehensive introduction to a particular group of people. What is the history of that group in America? What is the diversity within the group? What are the unique mental, physical, or socioeconomic issues associated with the group? It is important to acknowledge that many cultural variations exist within ethnic communities. Knowing how different cultural groups approach health as well as having a better understanding of how factors such as acculturation are important and how lifestyle decisions are made, can help clinicians, health care workers, and others be more culturally competent. The efforts to increase cultural competency in the treatment of mental and physical health are promising, but the wider health care arena and the general public need to pay attention to the causes of health disparities and the role played by multicultural approaches to health. We need a better connection between health care and the community, so individuals can seek out treatments that best fit their cultural needs and manifold health disparities can be reduced.

Regan A. R. Gurung
Ben J. and Joyce Rosenberg Professor of Human
Development and Psychology
University of Wisconsin, Green Bay

Preface

As I considered how to structure this book and what information to include, I realized the complexity and variety of topics necessary to fully cover the subject of Mexican American psychology was vast. Because of this, the book is somewhat unorthodox. I omitted several topics and shortened chapters, as the full content would require several volumes. I organized the book into two major sections. The first is related to social and anthropological topics to provide a general background about the Mexican American population and some of the theories that come with understanding this population. Several chapters describe traditions and customs and provide an overview of the typical lifestyle of this population. Although the content of this section is not clinical, it is essential to becoming a culturally competent clinician for this population. The second section addresses clinical issues.

Part I

Introduction to Sociological and Anthropological Topics

Chapter 1

Overview of Mexican American Psychology

In the spring of 2010, while at a conference in Dallas, I ventured downtown for lunch. Since Dallas is home to one of the largest Mexican populations in the United States (Ennis, Rios-Vargas, and Albert, 2011), I chose Mexican fare. At a gray building with a large "Mexican Food" sign, the owner spoke both English and Spanish and explained that the restaurant had a wide variety of Mexican dishes as well as foods from other ethnic and cultural groups. I recognized some dishes based by appearance and ingredients, but their names were unfamiliar. Others I had never been exposed to before. I ordered ground beef with potatoes (known as *picadillo*) and talked with the owner about how many variations within Mexican cuisine exist. To my surprise, he did not know much about this because he was from Guatemala. His customers did not know the difference between Mexican or Guatemalan food, so he called everything Mexican food as that was more profitable for him.

I share this story to make a couple of points regarding perceptions of Mexican culture. Although several similarities exist among Latin American cultures, specific features distinguish each. Unfortunately, because of several factors discussed in this book, we are often not successful in identifying features that differentiate one culture from another, and we generalize groups based on their similarities, leading clinicians and other professionals to believe the same behavior can be expected from all. The aim of this book is to examine Mexican American culture from different perspectives, to provide an overview of characteristics of this culture, and to present how this culture differs from others in the United States. In having this knowledge, we can avoid inaccurate generalizations and appreciate this culture and its members, which will result in more effective mental health treatment for this group.

People with different characteristics may adopt the designation *Mexican American* as a social, cultural, and ethnic identification (Gonzalez-Barrera and Lopez, 2013). In general, Mexican Americans are individuals who permanently migrated from Mexico, or those born in the United States (Gonzalez-Barrera and Lopez, 2013) whose parents, grandparents, or great-grandparents were born in Mexico. Most Mexican Americans reside in the western part of the United States (52 percent), particularly in California (about 36 percent). The southern part of the United States also has a high concentration of Mexican Americans, primarily in Texas, where 26 percent of the population resides (Gonzalez-Barrera and Lopez, 2013).

This book presents Mexican American psychology from different perspectives. This topic has not always been addressed as an independent field, and a term like *Chicano psychology* has been used to incorporate the understanding of the field of psychology. Descriptions of this population usually do not cover all the groups that could be considered Mexican American. To apply the information effectively, it is important to understand sociocultural, linguistic, and clinical factors.

THE MEXICAN AMERICAN POPULATION

The Mexican American population constitutes one of our largest minority groups and is rapidly growing due to several factors. This group is considered part of the general classification Hispanic, which includes people of Cuban descent, those from Puerto Rico, Central or South America, or other cultures with Spanish roots, and does not include any racial characteristics (United States Census Bureau, 2013). According to the 2010 U.S. Census, the Hispanic population grew 43 percent, while the general population grew only 10 percent. The Hispanic group that grew the most was the Mexican American population, which grew 54 percent in the past 10 years. That constitutes 31.8 million people, excluding those not included in the census, such as undocumented immigrants.

With this recent population increase, it is important to develop new scholarly sources that provide extensive and detailed information about the characteristics of this group and the differences among individuals who may be socially classified as Mexican Americans. Understanding the level of acculturation, assimilation, and linguistic characteristics, and knowing clinically appropriate interventions, is imperative for appropriate implementation and application of services to this population.

To understand better the origin and purpose of Mexican American psychology, it is important to review the origin and development of three important movements within the field of psychology: cultural psychology, cross-cultural psychology, and indigenous psychology.

ORIGINS OF CULTURAL PSYCHOLOGY

During the establishment of the field of psychology as a recognized academic and scholarly area of study, little emphasis was placed on culture and its possible impact on human behavior. Other fields, however, began to expand their knowledge about culture and how it should be utilized in the social sciences. To explore the origins of the subfield of cultural psychology and how this concept became essential in the social sciences, we need to look at the field of anthropology, which can be summarized as "the systematic study of humankind" (Scupin, 2012, p. 2). Because the term *humankind* is broad, all social sciences do this in one way or another. The significant difference in anthropology is that it incorporates four perspectives, or subfields, allowing the combination of information from the natural sciences, the humanities, and the social sciences for a general understanding of the past and the present of humankind (Scupin, 2012). The four subfields are physical/biological anthropology, archaeology, linguistic anthropology, and cultural anthropology.

Franz Boas and Cultural Relativism

The original purpose of developing a field such as anthropology was to study and understand non-Western cultures (Scupin, 2012). This approach led researchers to immediately compare those cultures with what was established in the West, resulting in ethnocentrism or viewing such cultures as inferior by judging and analyzing according to Western societies' standards (Scupin, 2012).

It was not until Franz Boas established the concept of cultural relativism that people began to appreciate cultural differences in a less dominant and competitive manner. Boas, considered by many to be the founder of American anthropology (Moore, 2012), proposed that instead of comparing cultures according to the perspective of one, all cultures should be viewed and analyzed according to their own characteristics and should not be compared to determine which ones are better or worse (Scupin, 2012). With this premise, he further expanded this theory by establishing that cultures are only more or less complex from one another. Even though a certain required comparison is necessary in this analysis, it did not require some cultures to be superior to others (Moore, 2012; Scupin, 2012).

Boas was born and raised in Germany and studied physics, mathematics, and geography. He studied under Wilhelm Wundt, who established the first psychology laboratory (Mattingly, Lutkehaus, and Throop, 2008). The merging of interests between psychology and anthropology was already present in some settings. For example, one of Wundt's research interests was *volkerpsychologie*, or folk psychology, which attempted to provide psychological explanations for cultural phenomena (Mattingly *et al.*, 2008). After obtaining his doctorate in physics, Boas became interested in studying human cultures and societies and did some work with the Inuit in Canada. This work influenced him to study culture and to change the face of contemporary anthropology (Moore, 2012).

Several examples in contemporary society can be used to depict the importance of cultural relativism, primarily because of the complexity of social and cultural variables. Food is one of these. In South Texas, in an area known as the Rio Grande Valley, it is quite common to find bakeries and other food stores selling *barbacoa*, a traditional Mexican dish made from different parts of a cow, including the tongue. Most people in this region have at least tried this dish, but people from other regions may not find it appealing. A person from a different cultural and social background in which it is not customary to eat this type of food may prefer not to eat it or may even find it difficult to believe such food can be eaten. From a culturally relativistic perspective, this practice should not be viewed from another culture's lens and should not be judged by the other culture's standards and expectations. This practice should be viewed within the context of the culture that enforces it.

Cultural Psychology

Cultural relativism and the influence of culture in human behavior were not always appreciated in the field of psychology. The work of cognitive psychologist Jerome Bruner allowed for cultural factors to be appreciated and considered when analyzing behavior (Tharp, 2007). Bruner appreciated the study of culture through anthropology and incorporated a lot of this field's concepts into his work (Tharp, 2007). His influence led to the development of the subfield of cultural psychology, which incorporates elements of psychology and anthropology and analyzes the interaction between an individual's mind and elements of a person's life as a member of society, such as law, morals, and art (Bruner, 2005). Cultural psychology also includes the analysis of human mental processes' connection to elements of institutions and the background of the individual (Santamaria, Cubero, and De la Mata, 2010).

Researchers in contemporary cultural psychology have addressed the importance of folk medical traditions in a person's development as a member of any group (Sue and Sue, 2012). Furthermore, the understanding of other cultures according to their own characteristics has been fundamental for psychologists trained in a primarily Western system (Lonner and Adamopoulos, 1997). The area of cultural psychology that addresses a relativistic approach to behavior is known as *indigenous psychology*, defined by Berry and Kim (1993) as the area of study that analyzes human behavior and mental processes in a systematic manner from a relativistic approach. It considers that elements within a culture should not be judged as superior or inferior, but should be seen as unique characteristics (Berry and Kim, 1993). The analysis is based only on the location where the behavior is observed, on the behavior that is exclusively local and does not migrate, and on the cultural variables created by members of that society.

Although some scholars believe indigenous psychology should create a universal psychology in which practitioners and scholars understand general cultural influences on behavior across cultures (Berry and Kim, 1993), some scholars believe it is better to understand and treat each culture with singularity and individualism (Tharp, 2007).

The subfield of *cultural psychology* is an emerging area of study (Tharp, 2007). Its origins resulted from work by anthropologists and psychologists focused on establishing the importance of cultural aspects in human behavior. However, due to several obstacles such as defining culture as a single and widely accepted concept and incorporating this definition across several social sciences, this field has struggled to be recognized and be influential in academic and clinical settings (Mattingly *et al.*, 2008; Tharp, 2007). Even in contemporary psychology, traditional theories fail to consider cultural factors (Rothbaum, Weisz, Pott, Miyake, and Morelli, 2001).

Some scholars have attempted, in a variety of ways, to combine psychology and the study of culture and fields that attempt to study culture, such as anthropology. Some people have used related areas such as philosophy to try to establish a relationship (Tharp, 2007). The skepticism by some scholars to utilize cultural components in mental health and psychology has made these attempts difficult (Tharp, 2007). Although opposition exists toward the development of cultural psychology, some scholars are interested in seeing the concepts applied to other specialties (Mattingly *et al.*, 2008; Tharp, 2007; O'Donnell, 2006).

Some academics believe in the understanding of cultural influences but do not believe it is possible to elaborate upon a universal psychology (Tharp, 2007), opposing what was proposed by Berry and others, who consider that it is essential to attempt to understand people from their own cultural perspective and context (Berry and Kim, 1993). In spite of these beliefs, most scholars agree that the behavior of individuals is the result of a mix of variables such as individual differences, the background and culture of the individual, and the situation the person faces as the behavior takes place (Smith, Spillane, and Annus, 2006).

Regardless of the opinions of scholars in this area, the influence of culture cannot be discredited. But what does cultural psychology entail? Because culture is a term that has been defined in several different ways, describing cultural psychology can be equally as complex (Tharp, 2007). According to Bruner, cultural psychology is the subfield that incorporates elements of psychology and anthropology or the area that analyzes the interaction between an individual's mind and elements of the life of that individual acquired as a member of society, such as law, morals, and art (Bruner, 2005). Cultural psychology also includes the analysis of how human mental processes are connected to elements of institutions and the background of the individual (Santamaria *et al.*, 2010). Also, as opposed to other related areas, cultural psychology researchers tend to study cultures that are very different from their own (Triandis, 2000).

The Merging of Culture and Psychology

During the 19th century, several academic areas began to flourish. Fields such as anthropology, biology, and psychology were being established, and though each explored different dimensions, it was apparent some elements were influential across disciplines and that learning about them could only allow for their particular discipline to grow (Mattingly *et al.*, 2008). Early psychologists and anthropologists experienced this phenomenon and decided to share concepts about personality, culture, and human development as experienced in different societies (Mattingly *et al.*, 2008).

Even though it was common to find academics sharing knowledge across other disciplines, the establishment of cultural psychology did not formally begin until a movement began by psychologists emphasizing cultural values in personality and behavior and a recognition of how personality and individual differences could be affected by—or could affect—a person's interpretation and function as a member of society who is following cultural norms (Mattingly *et al.*, 2008).

One of the earliest psychologists to address the importance of culture and to help establish cultural psychology was Jerome Bruner, a major proponent of cognitive psychology. As mentioned, Bruner believes that to understand human behavior, one must consider culture before biology (Mattingly *et al.*, 2008). This concept was not well accepted in the 19th century by scientists who believed in the importance of biological predisposition in human development. However, it was clear that to create awareness of culture, it was necessary to incorporate several areas of study (Mattingly *et al.*, 2008).

At this point, psychologists and anthropologists influenced each other in further developing their fields. For example, the contributions of several of Wundt's students made a significant impact on the field of anthropology. Bronislaw Malinowski utilized information from his work with a matrilineal culture (Trobriand Islanders) to challenge Freud's Oedipus complex theory (Mattingly *et al.*, 2008).

As some psychologists began to pay more attention to culture, anthropologists began to focus more on personality and its influence. In the 1920s, Edward Sapir, who became interested in the influence of cognitive psychology in anthropology, prepared a series of classes and seminars about psychology, culture, and personality (Mattingly *et al.*, 2008).

In the 1930s, Sapir and other anthropologists became interested in incorporating concepts of psychology and psychiatry into their area of study. They held multidisciplinary meetings to address the influence and relatedness of these fields (Mattingly *et al.*, 2008). While these meetings occurred, Lev Vygotsky in the Soviet Union proposed a different type of theory of cognition that involved the importance of social and cultural factors in human development. Vygotsky called this theory the *sociocultural cognitive theory* in which he suggested that for people to grow, develop, and learn, they must be guided by learning things they are able to learn according to their age, stage of development, and experiences. Vygotsky called this the zone of proximal development (Santrock, 2007).

Vygotsky's theory was not considered a grand theory (Berger, 2016). While it attempted to establish the importance of social and cultural factors in development, other theories focused on the individual. For example, Piaget proposed his cognitive development theory, which suggests children are able to learn and perceive their surroundings by going through four stages of development (Santrock, 2007).

Bruner, being a cognitive psychologist, was familiar with both Vygotsky and Piaget's theories. He considered Vygotsky's idea in some ways more valuable than Piaget's because of the incorporation of guidance and social cultural factors in learning. However, he and his graduate students were not able to experience Vygotsky's theory with other cultures until the 1960s, when they traveled to conduct research in Africa, particularly Senegal, and Alaska (Mattingly *et al.*, 2008). The results were published in Bruner's book, *Studies in Cognitive Growth* (Mattingly *et al.*, 2008), allowing for both anthropology and psychology to interact again, and serving as a milestone in the establishment of cultural psychology (Mattingly *et al.*, 2008).

Some scholars suggest two other major events in Bruner's life shaped him and led him to perceive the importance of a field such as cultural psychology (Lutkehaus, 2008). The first was his role in the creation of *Man, A Course of Study* (MACC), which was an introductory anthropology curriculum created for elementary school children (Lutkehaus, 2008). The other was his involvement in the development of the federal program Head Start under the administration of Lyndon B. Johnson (Lutkehaus, 2008).

In a recent article, Bruner shared his concerns about problems with the development of cultural psychology and several unsuccessful attempts to combine psychology and anthropology. Although he believed psychologists should be sensitive to cultural variables, he thought it was almost impossible to establish a universal psychology because each culture possesses unique characteristics. Nonetheless, Bruner believed in understanding both individual mental processes and culture for further scholarly development. He proposed three ways in which culture influenced the mind: First, culture allows society to create an understanding of what is normal and to create the social establishments that tell us what is acceptable and what is abnormal. Second, culture sets boundaries and forms our understanding of the things that are real and doable while limiting our understanding of the things that are possible. Finally, culture gives individuals ways to interrelate what is normal and what is doable by narrative conventions (Bruner, 2005).

Additionally, Bruner related three dilemmas that arose after he analyzed the relationship between culture and individual processes of the mind:

The first dilemma arises when we ask how to study the human condition. Is man, indeed, the proper study of mankind, as Alexander Pope urged, or had we better consider man in the social settings that provide him his identity, shape his desires, and even forge his destiny? The answer is that we must do both.

The second dilemma is related. Shall we take man as the agent of his acts (as we mostly do in Anglo-American law) or is he the "victim" of circumstances, the "output" of a social system, or what? Obviously, the two approaches (while irreconcilable) enrich each other.

Third, granting that man in some measure expresses the culture of which he is a member, how shall we conceive of the interaction? How does culture come to have such an influence on man's inner personal experience as well as on his acts? This dilemma, of course, is old hat in both psychology and anthropology—yet, it is as unresolved as ever. Yet, both fields are enriched by its challenge. (Bruner, 2005, p. 61)

Another important aspect regarding how the fields of anthropology and psychology merged to bring cultural psychology into existence is the role of meaning on sociocultural aspects of life. Every aspect of culture represents something in a person's cognition because the person assigns meaning to such variables. Cultural elements have to be perceived by the person's psyche in order to mean something to the person (Shweder, 1990).

Research in Cultural Psychology

Several perspectives can be considered pertaining to cultural research in Western society. Some people have attempted to create awareness of cultural values and multiculturalism (Berry, 2001; Draguns, 2008; Sue and Sue, 2012); however, some of these research studies have important limitations. Researchers on multiculturalism often do not identify and consider variations within a given group. For example, research that utilizes participants of Asian ancestry sometimes fails to include all factions that are part of this group. It may include participants from Chinese, Korean, and Japanese ancestry, but if it fails to include people from India, the Philippines, and other Asian countries, the results cannot be generalized to all people of Asian descent (Erard, 2009; Kim and Sherman, 2009).

Furthermore, critics of cultural psychology research tend to identify such studies as biased and full of stereotypes of ethnic groups (Kim and Sherman, 2009). Researchers in cultural psychology argue it would not be possible to include every cultural group (Kim and Sherman, 2009). Additionally, they consider culture more than nationality (Kim and Sherman, 2009). Culture includes several variables such as socioeconomic status and religion. Therefore, when conducting cultural research and defining cultural groups, one must consider different variables, and studies should not consider only national origin (Kim and Sherman, 2009). Ultimately, the purpose of cultural psychology research is to analyze and discover diverse ways of behaving as influenced by culture. Another purpose is to show the varieties of psychology experienced by different humans in different contexts (Kim and Sherman, 2009).

Researchers in cultural psychology also have expressed concern about a lack of cultural sensitivity when conducting research in the United States, and that is often generalized to the rest of the world (Haeffel, Thiessen, Campbell, Kaschak, and McNeil, 2009). Additionally, some researchers recommend conducting research that considers the context of the behavior of the individual and the cultural background of the person (Arnett, 2008). This recommendation is not always well accepted by American psychologists who consider some human elements and behaviors to be universal, to an extent. Hence, some research could be generalized (Haeffel *et al.*, 2009). Furthermore, applying cultural sensitivity to research conducted in the United States suggests that psychologists should change their approach, threatening basic research such as classic obedience studies, which allowed psychology to understand human abuses (Haeffel *et al.*, 2009).

Another limitation is that the researchers in this field do not include quantitative data from laboratory studies. Instead, they consider mainly qualitative information gathered from ethnographic research methods, which do not occur as frequently in cross-cultural psychology and may hinder obtaining the most accurate results (Triandis, 2000).

Cultural Psychology versus Cross-Cultural Psychology

Interchangeable use of cultural and cross-cultural psychology is common. Although these terms are related and may overlap with each other and with indigenous psychology, they vary in research methodologies, purposes, and objectives (Greenfield, 2000). Berry (2000) has suggested that understanding cultural values and variables is necessary when studying human behavior and must come about before considering cross-cultural psychology.

Cultural psychology also regards culture as within the person rather than outside of him or her and considers an approach to problems and research questions by looking at the nature of the culture (Greenfield, 2000).

Origins of Cross-Cultural Psychology

In 1972, the International Association for Cross-Cultural Psychology (IACCP) gathered for the first time. It was established by scholars who resided in areas that used to be part of the British Empire and who began to detect cultural differences and their influence on people's behaviors. Aware of such differences, scholars believed they had the professional and academic responsibility of exploring how other cultures varied from their own (Greenfield, 2000).

Cross-cultural psychology systematically studies any possible relationships among variables related to the development of humans, their culture, and their behaviors associated with the culture (Berry, 1997). Unlike cultural psychology, in cross-cultural psychology, culture is viewed as independent from the individual (Greenfield, 2000). This field is characterized by the research methods it uses (Laungani, 2002), which usually consist of quantitative data from several cultural groups, and explores the interaction and relationship of variables among these cultures (Triandis, 2000). Cultural psychology researchers ignore individual differences and focus primarily on the culture, whereas cross-cultural psychology researchers place emphasis on individual differences and how different cultures impact these differences (Triandis, 2000). Cross-cultural psychology research uses a higher number of established Western theories (Greenfield, 2000). Furthermore, the research on cultural psychology is usually conducted by men of European ancestry outside the United States, and when data from the United States is included, it is compared with that of other countries in an attempt to generalize the results (Nagayama Hall and Maramba, 2001). By contrast, research in some specialty areas in cultural psychology, such as ethnic minority psychology, is only conducted in the United States (Nagayama Hall and Maramba, 2001).

When conducting studies in cross-cultural psychology, researchers need to be aware not only of the different languages spoken, but also of cultural variations in order to avoid misleading data (Lee, Li, Arai, and Puntillo, 2009).

Individualism versus Collectivism

A major area of interest in cultural and cross-cultural psychology research is the perception of individualism and collectivism and how they vary according to culture (Sue and Sue, 2012). Individualism is an orientation in which the person's individual objectives are most important and the person is favored over the person's surrounding system, including family and friends (Santrock, 2007). Persons with this orientation highly value independence and autonomy as well as the individual responsibility of making decisions for his or her own benefit (Sue and Sue, 2012).

In contrast, a collectivistic orientation is one in which the group is viewed as most important (Santrock, 2007). Personal objectives and individualism are not valued more than group prosperity (Santrock, 2007). Understanding these different orientations is crucial to adequate clinical interventions (Sue and Sue, 2012). For example, a person from an individualistic orientation is more likely to experience guilt, while people from collectivistic cultures are more likely to experience shame, placing emphasis on their sensitivity toward a group (Sue and Sue, 2012).

Research in these two areas began in and progressively increased since 1980, when organizational sociologists from the Netherlands started investigating their influence in workplace goals in 40 countries (Hwang, 2005b). Since then, several other instruments of varying effectiveness, depending on the setting and purpose, have attempted to measure these cultural orientations. A recent study showed that Triandis' Horizontal and Vertical Individualism and Collectivism scale appeared more effective in evaluating these constructs (Paquet and Kline, 2009). In general terms, the Mexican American population is collectivistic. This is important, particularly when working with this population in a clinical setting (Sue and Sue, 2012).

Etic and Emic Approaches

In cultural and cross-cultural psychology, one of the most important concepts borrowed from anthropology is the etic and emic approaches of analysis (Sue and Sue, 2012). Etic refers to universalities or things that are supposed to occur across cultures. The emic perspective is a culture-specific approach. These concepts are essential in contemporary mental health (Sue and Sue, 2012). The diagnoses and treatment methods are often assumed to be universal and, therefore, a single model of treatment should be effective across cultures. Nevertheless, research has shown some elements are specific to the culture of the individual (Sue and Sue, 2012). Cultural and cross-cultural psychology research is believed to lie between both etic and emic perspectives (Triandis, 2000).

Anthropology, however, had had a more universalistic approach before Boas presented his theories. His training as a student of Wundt in Germany (Mattingly *et al.*, 2008) allowed him to propose the concept of cultural relativism, which suggests that anthropologists should analyze and understand any culture according to its own characteristics (Ember, Ember, and Peregrine, 2014), and cultures should not be compared. Instead of researchers considering some cultures to be superior to others, Boas proposed researchers view cultures as either more or less complex than others (Ember *et al.*, 2014).

Indigenous Psychology

The presence of etic and emic approaches of analysis in cultural and cross-cultural psychology has allowed for a new area of study to emerge: indigenous psychology. This subfield is defined as the systematic analysis of human behavior and mental processes that is local, does not migrate, and is created by members of a particular society (Berry and Kim, 1993). It has also been proposed that its practicality involves the analysis of local behaviors and that this is understood according to the characteristics of the culture—in other words, cultural relativism (Adair, 1999).

As opposed to cultural and cross-cultural psychology, indigenous psychology is believed to be a primarily emic approach (Triandis, 2000). It is considered to be the way in which psychologists from non-Western cultures attempt to deal with the dominance of Western psychology by encouraging attention to culture and context in psychological research (Hwang, 2005b). Some people considered this movement to contain elements of anti-imperialism and anti-colonialism (Hwang, 2005a). Since Western psychology has been designed to study and analyze populations from a universalist perspective, it is assumed that its methods and approaches will work in any part of the world. Nevertheless, people from non-Western countries have applied these principles and realized the concepts proposed by Western psychology do not necessarily apply to non-Western countries (Hwang, 2005a).

Indigenous psychology evolved from the development of cultural psychology (Hwang, 2005b). Although research at the end of the 1970s in non-Western countries such as Japan, Korea, Mexico, the Philippines, and India analyzed psychological processes, it was in the 1990s when indigenous psychology became legitimate and people began to seriously conduct research using its concepts (Hwang, 2005b). Recent research has included China, Taiwan, Papua New Guinea, New Zealand, and Cameroon as well as areas in the United States, Canada, Sweden, and Poland (Allwood and Berry, 2006).

Although research in indigenous psychology has commonalities with cultural psychology, substantial differences can be found. For example, cultural psychology research establishes psychological ethnic theories but does not test them in single, specific cultures. Indigenous psychology researchers test these theories (Greenfield, 2000).

Although some discrepancies exist in the definition and application of indigenous psychology, common characteristics can be found among researchers (Triandis, 2000).

The main advantage of indigenous psychology research is that it allows psychologists to fully understand a single culture and its characteristics, which may not be present in other cultures (Triandis, 2000). It also allows people who study particular cultures to obtain data that can serve as the basis for the development of theories and will help in the understanding of that culture (Triandis, 2000).

Psychologists in other specialties consider the field to be the same as anthropology and have criticized indigenous psychology as leading to the inability to consider important elements that may require a broader approach (Hwang, 2005b; Triandis, 2000). Also, because of variability within a specific cultural group, the results of research may be quite different and, in some cases, even contradictory (Triandis, 2000).

Supporters of indigenous psychology support breaking with Western psychology's scientific ethnocentrism, but warn it is as important not to fall into culture-specific scientific ethnocentrism, as it may lead to the ignoring of important variables (Hwang, 2005a).

The development of the areas of cultural psychology, cross-cultural psychology, and indigenous psychology has allowed scholars to focus on the importance of cultural factors in human behavior, and vice versa. The bases of these fields allow for the field of psychology to study different groups, including the Mexican American population, from a relativistic perspective, taking into account cultural characteristics and avoiding imposing a

Western perspective on characteristics that need to be considered as independent and unique.

WHAT WILL BE COVERED IN THIS BOOK

Because of the complexity of the Mexican American population's cultural characteristics, understanding this population from different perspectives will better equip practitioners. Understanding the origins and concepts of cultural, cross-cultural, and indigenous psychology permit the reader to analyze this book from different perspectives, thus acquiring a thorough vision of the characteristics of the Mexican American population.

The first part of the book will include social and cultural topics, such as contemporary characteristics of Mexican Americans and their history, current social issues like immigration, and language. The second part will incorporate clinical topics to keep in mind when working with this population, including factors that need to be considered when conducting a Mental Status Exam, performing crisis intervention, or completing a psychological assessment or evaluation.

Chapter 2

Mexican American History

When I was an adolescent, my family was invited to a reunion after my uncle put together a family tree tracking members back to the early 1840s when South Texas was still part of Mexico. Family members spoke with pride of being descendants of the Mexicans first involved in becoming part of the United States. They seemed particularly proud that they did not have to migrate to the United States, but the United States migrated toward them. They identified as Mexican Americans, but expressed pride as American citizens. The tone of the conversation changed, however, when younger family members said they were not Mexican because they were born in the United States, even stressing they did not speak Spanish. One of the oldest members of the family, who spoke both English and Spanish, waited until the youngsters finished and said, "You say you are not Mexican, but yet you celebrate Cinco de Mayo . . . in an American way and without knowing what you are celebrating, but you still celebrate it."

Mexican American history is as diverse as the people who forged it. Because it is complex and cannot be defined simply by looking at a particular region of the United States in which Mexican Americans have lived for some time, we cannot talk about Mexican American history without including some Mexican and American history. We will first cover briefly the origins of Mexico, followed by events that involve both Mexico and the United States and that allowed for both the division and integration of Mexicans in the United States. Chapter 3 will cover the recent history of Mexican Americans who have set a path toward contemporary Mexican American society. This information helps explain current cultural practices and characteristics of Mexican American culture.

THE ORIGIN OF MEXICO

Before we can talk about Mexican American history, we need to go back to the origins of Mexico. Numerous cultures populated parts of what is now Mexico. There are several theories of how people migrated to the Americas, including what is now known as Mexico. Some propose that people traveled through the oceans (Rothman, 2016). One popular theory suggests the first settlers (particularly to North and Central America) arrived from Eurasia after crossing the Bering Strait during the Pleistocene epoch, also known as the Ice Age (Rothman, 2016). After crossing into the northern part of the Americas, they traveled south. Some established settlements throughout North America, and others migrated until they reached the region known as Mesoamerica, which divides the two greater pieces of land of the American continent: North America and South America (Coe and Koontz, 2002). Mesoamerica generally includes the central part of Mexico and Panama, Guatemala, Belize, Nicaragua, El Salvador, Costa Rica, and Honduras (Huber, 2001; Morehart and Morell-Hart, 2015).

Early settlers were primarily hunters and gatherers, but as they established communities, they began to incorporate agricultural practices (Coe and Koontz, 2002). From these establishments, many cultures were developed, starting with the Olmec civilization, which is considered to be the oldest ancient Mexican civilization, dating back to 1700 B.C.E. (Coe and Koontz, 2002). Other cultures also formed part of Mexico throughout the years, including the Zapotec, the Mayan Empire, in the southern part of Mexico and Guatemala, and the Toltec civilization, which was the precursor to the Aztec Empire (Coe and Koontz, 2002).

Aztec Civilization

Although each ancient civilization that resided in what is now Mexico is important and influenced contemporary cultural practices to some extent, the Aztec Empire was the most influential, particularly as the last pre-Columbian civilization before the Spanish invasion (Coe and Koontz, 2002). This culture was also powerful and important to different societal developments such as an economy, a military, religion, and advancements in mathematics and other essential knowledge for humankind.

According to Aztec mythology, the forefathers of the Aztec Empire migrated from a place called *Aztlan*, a Nahuatl word that means Land of White Herons. The settlers there were advised by Huitzilopochtli, their tribal god who also was considered to represent the sun and warfare, to migrate to the location where they would establish their new home (Levin Rojo, 2014). Legend states Huitzilopochtli asked them to travel until they found an eagle standing in a cactus, devouring a snake. They walked south for a long time, eventually finding the symbol in the middle of Lake Texcoco and settling there (Smith, 1984). Since the eagle and the cactus were in the lake, they developed a way to place floating ground over the water. This ground was known as *chinampas*, which literally means floating gardens. However, this ground was not only to plant or cultivate, but also to set solid ground to establish a sedentary community (Armillas, 1971). They called their city Tenochtitlan.

Tenochtitlan was considered a metropolis and the center of Aztec culture. When the Spanish conquistadores arrived in Mesoamerica, the Aztec Empire had expanded and governed a wide range surrounding Tenochtitlan. Educational institutions and an economic and political structure allowed them solvency (Coe and Koontz, 2002), but they fought with rival groups such as the Tlaxcaltecs and Huexotzincans (Leon-Portilla, 1963).

In order to thoroughly understand the Aztec Empire's practices, customs, and influence in contemporary society, it is crucial to analyze present practices in Mexico, especially where indigenous people still have not been impacted by Western societies, as seen in the predominance of their native ancient languages and dialects (e.g., the Zapotecs, Mixtecs, Yucatec Mayans, and Nahuatls) (Faudree, 2015). Current practices can help us understand the impact of Aztec culture in today's society.

SIMILARITIES BETWEEN AZTEC AND CONTEMPORARY SOCIETY

Contrary to popular belief, several customs practiced in contemporary Mexican and Mexican American societies can be traced to pre-Columbian times. Some of these customs have adapted over time, while others maintain their original characteristics. The following are some of these practices and aspects of society that have an ancient origin.

Food

Nutrition is an important element in the analysis of pre-Columbian Mesoamerica, specifically the Aztec Empire and contemporary Mexico. As a result of several archaeological investigations and even images and illustrations in several sources, it is known that the Aztec, like other Mesoamerican cultures, had maize, chili, beans, and squash as a major nutritional base. A contemporary Mexican family diet is also mainly composed of beans and maize. One of the most well-known foods in the region are tortillas made of maize or corn. In contemporary Mexico and in con-temporary Mexican American U.S. communities, it is very common to find people in line waiting to buy tortillas by the kilo (Heath, 1987) at tortillerías where they are made and sold.

Beans are also extremely important to the diet of Mexicans. They are a source of protein and often very affordable, which brings us to the impor-tance of labor in the fields for both contemporary Mexicans and pre-Columbian Aztecs. Because it is essential to have maize and beans in the Mexican and Aztec diets, it is necessary to have individuals who work exclu-sively on agriculture. The surrounding areas of the Valley of Mexico serve as agricultural fields. Unfortunately, with globalization and the incorpora-tion of free markets into North America as well as customs and practices brought to Mexico by the Spaniards, the compensation for harvesting the food has been devaluated (Peña, Villalobos, Martinez, Sotelo, Gil, and Delgado-Salinas, 1999). Some of the agricultural sites in Mexico were also utilized by Aztec people in pre-Columbian times. They are often located in rural areas surrounding the major cities of Central Mexico, such as Cuer-navaca, Morelos, and even Mexico City (Smith, Aguirre, Heath-Smith, Hirst, O'Mack, and Price, 1989).

Market System

The market system established within a culture and among different groups was essential in the development of different aspects of Aztec soci-ety. This system was complex and based on several economic concepts that can be found in today's Mexican economic system.

Trade and exchange of goods was common, and the utilization of valu-able items as currency was also fundamental. Things such as cacao beans, jade, and obsidian were worth more than other things. Jade and cacao were considered symbols of nobility among many Mesoamerican civilizations, whereas obsidian, which is volcanic glass, was valued as a major material to create sharp tools for the battlefield or for other activities such as cut-ting meat. Tenochtitlan, the capital city of the Aztec Empire, was not a pre-dominant producer of jade or obsidian, but they were often imported from other local sites such as Teotihuacan (Spence, 1967).

The culture of Teotihuacan collapsed before the beginning of the Aztec Empire. However, this site remained a religious center and market where possibly several groups gathered together to sell and trade goods. Items such as obsidian were probably brought to Tenochtitlan and other sites of the Aztec Empire from Teotihuacan (Spence, 1967).

In the central area of Mexico, more specifically near Tenochtitlan in the Aztec Empire, the market system consisted of the production of goods outside the major city and the selling of such products in several markets, the majority being inside Tenochtitlan. Items from different places were considered valuable, but the market system predominately sold essential goods and food from the producers. Within Tenochtitlan and its surrounding cities and sites, canals transported these goods into the markets. The Aztec natives were aware of such market days and made arrangements to sell or buy goods on the days these markets were open (Rojas Gonzalez, 1945).

In contemporary Mexico, markets similar to those found in pre-Columbian times also take place on certain days, and although several items are sold, many people purchase agricultural goods that are cheaper than at a supermarket. The term to describe these markets is *tianguis*, which comes from the nahuatl *tianquiztli* and means market or public place (Rojas Gonzalez, 1945). In the United States, flea markets follow a similar pattern. For example, in parts of the United States such as Texas and California, similar markets, identified as *pulgas*, feature products such as fruits and vegetables, snacks, sweets, and prepared foods (Dean, Sharkey, and John, 2011).

City Structure and Division

The city of Tenochtitlan was the main center of the Aztec Empire. It was the capital city and the central location of religious ceremonies, economic activity, and nobles and governors. Even though there were other religious and social leaders in other Aztec populations, Tenochtitlan was predominant in the Aztec Empire (Mundy, 1998).

Within Tenochtitlan, subdivisions socially organized the city. These subdivisions, known as *calpulli* or *calpolli* (plural *calpultin*), were found in other parts of the Aztec Empire. Although simply a term to specify territorial divisions, the concept now refers to social organization divisions that include a group of families who have kinship, religious practices (i.e., a patron saint), and other social characteristics in common (Hicks, 1982).

The Aztec Empire had established several important cities around Tenochtitlan. These neighboring locations were important not only for social alliances, such as when a noble from one site married a noble from another to improve relations between both, but also for economic and military reasons (Ingham, 1971).

Tenochtitlan was divided into *calpultin*, established in four quadrants. Each was to an extent independent; however, they followed and respected Aztec traditions.

In contemporary Mexico, some of the kingdoms and *calpultin* can still be seen. The subdivisions within the great Tenochtitlan are still present in Mexico City. Some are now political divisions of the city, called *delegaciones*.

Just like in Aztec times, each region is predominantly ruled and governed by a greater structure. In Aztec times, the kingdoms had their own rulers and governmental structure but were mainly under the supervision and control of the Aztec capital. In today's Mexico City, these *delegaciones* have local government and representatives that form part of the greater city government system, which also belongs to a larger structure, the federal Mexican government (Ingham, 1971; Calnek, 1972).

The major social structures in Aztec times also had some subdivisions that, although smaller and under the supervision of a major controlling government, had practices of their own. Smaller social structures that maintain the major characteristics of the *calpultin* were known as *barrios*. The traditions and practices enforced and influenced by the *calpulli* in a particular *barrio* were seen as part of the social life of the general population. However, other practices specific to barrios had unique characteristics and characteristics from other regions influenced by the same *calpulli*. An analogy to this structure exists in contemporary Mexico. Each *delegacion* in Mexico City has some traditions and practices. For example, parties and celebrations within a *delegacion* are common and recognized by its members. In actuality, some of these practices are also recognized by people from other *delegaciones* invited to participate in them. Yet, other more centralized and specific celebrations are practiced within a *delegacion* and even within a still smaller division in this divided social structure. *Colonias* are also smaller structures that form *delegaciones*, often with specific traditions and celebrations that include individuals and residents from the specific *colonia* (Hayner and Montiel, 1964).

Within the *calpultin*, certain practices and traditions can be found in different central Mexican locations, particularly those that formed part of the Aztec Empire. However, such characteristics can also be found in other areas of the country that did not have major direct influence from Aztec society, such as in the north of Mexico. One of the most common of these characteristics is the presence of endogamous practices (Ingham, 1971). This practice can be the cause of a variety of behaviors, including mistrust from the members of a small community toward people from outside the community (Ingham, 1971).

Major differences between rural and urban characteristics in ancient Aztec times and in contemporary Mexico involve characteristics of people who lived in suburban areas adjacent to Tenochtitlan. In modern Mexico, the differences between those living in urban and rural areas can be the result of additional and more complex circumstances. However, the differences between both types of areas are noticeable in ancient Mexico as well as in today's Mexico.

Tenochtitlan

The great Tenochtitlan was a city described as magnificent and glorious. It had impressive temples and structures that left the Spanish conquistadors amazed and shocked that such a beautiful place could exist somewhere other than in their dreams (Coe and Koontz, 2002).

This site was the Aztec center of power in social institutions such as religion, the military, educational centers, and the economy. The major priests resided in this location along with the nobles and governors of the Aztec Empire. Even though there were other rulers and governors in surrounding areas of Tenochtitlan, they would mostly abide by the rules and norms established by the individuals from Tenochtitlan (Ingham, 1971).

In surrounding suburban sites, the population did not have access to the same types of services as the Aztec capital. Even though they were supposed to have the same social structure, the social differences in the suburban sites were noticeable. These sites had religious temples, their own military power, and even their own rulers and nobles. Although the economic trade system at that time allowed the inhabitants of suburban locations to be responsible for the production of their own goods, mainly agriculture and pottery, they were often guided to the Aztec capital to participate in the *tianguis* system because it increased the probability of a successful and convenient transaction (Rojas Gonzalez, 1945).

Additionally, residents of Tenochtitlan did not have immediate access to harvesting certain types of foods. Even though the production and handling of food directly from agriculture was common, the soil was not the same in Tenochtitlan as in other locations. Because Tenochtitlan was founded within a lake, a type of floating floor or garden was needed. These floating gardens were designed not only so a floor could eventually develop the capital city, but also so people could harvest plants often different from those in other types of fields (Calnek, 1972).

Discrimination

Because there were no major ethnic or sociocultural differences in pre-Columbian Aztec society, discrimination and prejudice were not likely common. The perception toward individuals from different sociocultural backgrounds who spoke different languages, however, could have been the result of negative attitudes.

Negative attitudes and the underrating of individuals were seen in social characteristics other than those related to ethnic background. For example, substantial evidence exists of how slaves and prisoners of war were viewed and treated. Sacrifices were conducted with these individuals, and they were considered inferior (Harner, 1977).

In contemporary Mexico, some of these characteristics are still found. They can be seen among people in different areas of the country with different characteristics, such as those who have moved to a major city from a rural area. The person's accent and skin color may be different from the region, which may elicit negative comments and discrimination. In today's Mexico, the center of the federal government is in Mexico City. Even though this city had a considerable number of people living there at the time the Spaniards arrived, today's population has resulted in Mexico City being considered one of the most populated cities in the world (Nortman, Halvas, and Rabago, 1986).

It is common to find people from suburban areas migrating to Mexico City to look for employment opportunities and to seek out education and even religion, as it has two of the most important institutions of public higher education, the *Instituto Politecnico Nacional* (National Polytechnic Institute) or *IPN*, and the *Universidad Nacional Autonoma de Mexico* (National Autonomous University of Mexico) or *UNAM*, as well as the most significant Mexican Catholic symbol, *La Basilica de Guadalupe*.

Since Mexico City is now one of the largest metropolises in the world, it is impossible for it to provide fields for agriculture. As a result, major differences exist between urban and rural areas in today's Mexico. Agriculture, although necessary, is not seen as prestigious. Instead, it is considered a weak occupational practice and an activity that should be conducted by illiterate individuals. It is also perceived that individuals in rural areas tend to have lower socioeconomic status than those in Mexico City (Rothstein, 1999).

Social Stratification

Evidence exists showing different social classes in several pre-Columbian cultures. Several elements portrayed and classified an individual's lifestyle and social status. For example, cacao was very valuable, and at one time only the elite and nobles were able to drink it in Mesoamerica. Additionally, remains of tombs across different sites display status according to their decorations. Some people were given a mask made of jade as a status symbol. Some of these royal tombs also contained pottery, murals, and other characteristics that honored the deceased individual (Coe and Koontz, 2002).

Specifically in the Aztec Empire, social differentiation was based on a variety of factors. The rulers or nobles and governors were the elite of the social Aztec organization. Warriors were considered important figures in the social ranking system. Priests and ceremonial leaders were also distinctive, as the Aztecs strongly believed in esoteric elements in their lifestyles. They had, like most Mesoamerican cultures, two calendars, one of which provided sacred information based on astrological observations and which allowed priests and religious leaders to make predictions as well as propose social activities and expectations (Ingham, 1971).

Another important aspect of social stratification in Aztec times is the distinction of activities between males and females. Gender distinction was crucial in the social organization and labor of the great Tenochtitlan. Some of the activities were determined by the nature of each gender. However, other more complex professions were designed specifically because of the cultural expectations and social characteristics of the Aztec Empire. The distinction between males and females was socially established, and formed part of the Aztec society. Deities and their characteristics were greatly influenced by the gender attributed to them. Some of the deities had dual characteristics. However, this duality had a particular objective. Others were assigned a gender because of their expected roles, functions, and divine characteristics (Mundy, 1998).

It was expected that the Aztec army could not include female warriors. Priests were also predominantly male. However, some activities were specifically for women. Midwives were essential in the Aztec Empire. They were, like today, in charge of assisting women in having children even though they usually did not work independently, as they needed to consult with priests about esoteric and astronomical matters (Kellogg, 1995).

Worth noting is the distinction of gender toward individuals who were captives from other regions as a result of warfare and for the purpose of sacrifices to honor the gods. Documented evidence exists that the Aztec Empire conducted sacrifices with captives, including children and adults of both genders. Even in some of these documents, the information presented shows males were expected to be strong and to avoid showing weakness (Carrasco, 1995).

In today's Mexican society, some similarities in attitudes toward status and gender differences can be seen. Social divisions are clearly marked. Individuals who are politically active and work in the government usually hold better socioeconomic positions. Material wealth also distinguishes status, which can be identified by the vehicle an individual drives, the size, characteristics, and location of the house the individual owns, and even the attire a person wears, such as gold items or brand names.

In addition, very apparent social distinctions exist. Although not always seen, women tend to stay home to raise children as males work to earn money. This arrangement appears more frequently in rural traditional communities than in urban establishments. The expectations of each gender are established according to social norms. For example, it is common to find women able to express their feelings, something that can be seen as a sign of weakness. This expression is rarely seen in males. The social expectation of contemporary Mexican males is that of being tough and strong, and women need to be tender to fulfill their social roles (O'nell, 1975).

Religion

A major element in the formation of today's Mexican society has been religion. This was also crucial in Aztec times. Religious practices and beliefs governed in some instances the general social living of the Aztecs. Calendar dates, astronomical observations, and even healing processes were linked to religion.

Religious myths and legends had been part of pre-Columbian societies. A very mystical figure, known as *Quetzalcoatl*, or the feathered serpent, was a main character in one of the most significant legends that helped shape the course of Aztec life. This deity left the predecessors of the Aztecs and said he would return on a date close to when Hernan Cortes arrived in Tenochtitlan to found New Spain. The completion of the conquest was not easy and included severe abuses on the part of the Spaniards toward the natives, but religious elements assisted in the transformation of a new culture (Zires, 1994).

The Aztec religion contained several deities, each with characteristics that made them unique and powerful in their own way. Most of these gods had male or female characteristics, while some consisted of a duality of gender (Mundy, 1998).

Some of the strongest and most influential deities had their own temple so that the general population could worship them. Several types of human sacrifices were conducted to worship and to please specific gods, such as Huitzilopochtli (Frank, 1989). A priest removed a person's heart in a ceremonial temple in front of the general population. Other sacrifices were self-mutilating behaviors, such as piercing body parts.

The Aztec priests had high social status and were recognized and consulted by members of society. Many social activities were based on the priest's astronomical observations and esoteric knowledge. Predictions were also made according to mythology and knowledge passed down from past generations (Coe and Koontz, 2002).

In Tenochtitlan and in other sites of the Aztec Empire, some religious traditions and festivities took place according to a calendar and with the purpose of celebrating a particular deity. Often, these deities were considered the patrons or guardians of specific sites, *barrios*, and *calpultin*. These practices were known by the town's people and were often characterized by the involvement of government officials, religious leaders, and the town's general population (Ingham, 1971).

Pilgrimage was also an important religious practice in Aztec times. Evidence exists of several examples across different stages of the Aztec Empire. For example, the Aztecs' guidance by Huitzilopochtli to find an eagle devouring a serpent on top of a cactus (Levin Rojo, 2014) shows movement of individuals from one location to another for spiritual and religious purposes.

This practice was also conducted later in the Aztec Empire. Since Teotihuacan was not populated at the time the Aztec Empire developed, it served as an instrument of enigmatic ideas and the site of ideas, according to the Aztec. For example, this site was named by the Aztec Empire as the city of the gods (Smith, 1984).

Evidence shows pilgrimages from the great Tenochtitlan to Teotihuacan as part of Aztec religious practices. Not only was this essential in Aztec life, but it was set as an example by their governor and ruler, Moctezuma, who performed such pilgrimages (Coe and Koontz, 2002).

After the Spaniards defeated the Aztec Empire and justified the conquest by using traditional customs of the Roman Catholic religion, the process of acculturation and the imposing of a new religion took place. After several pandemics wiped out approximately 90 percent of the native population and the Spanish army had conquered the Aztecs, the Aztecs had no choice but to abide by the rules of the invading army. Evangelization, according to the Spanish government, began to occur, while abuses toward the natives continued (Zeitlin and Thomas, 1992). Language barriers and cultural differences were important obstacles to overcome

As evangelization continued, the Spanish also needed to seek out gold and other valuables in accordance with European standards. Therefore, the transition to a new religion and a new language were extremely important in facilitating the change of power. A method the Spanish invaders utilized as part of acculturation was the adaptation of the previous Aztec religion into the new Catholic dogma. Thus, some similarities were emphasized and reinforced between the religions. For example, although the Catholic Church has one major god in the trinity, several other dogmatic characters exist called saints. Some were adapted according to the characteristics of local deities. An example is the moon goddess who was worshiped at a mountain and where later, at the hill site, Juan Diego, an indigenous native from New Spain after the conquest, communicated with the Virgin of Guadalupe (Zires, 1994).

Several of these characteristics are still found in contemporary Mexico. Some are the result of Spanish post-conquest intervention, while others can be traced to Aztec origins. For example, in the Catholic Church, several saints are remembered on days specifically dedicated to such saints. In some cases, saints are patrons of particular locations, and major festivities celebrate a city's patron saint. This practice takes place particularly in Spain (Ingham, 1971).

In pre-Columbian central Mexico, some *calpultin* and *barrios* conducted similar practices to venerate the deities that served as protectors of the location. Religious leaders, governmental officials, and the people of the town were represented, and in some festivities, spectators and visitors witnessed the traditional ceremonies.

Folk Medicine

Predominant world views of medicine and illness existed in Europe when the Spanish conquistadores arrived in the New World, and ancestral knowledge was important in Aztec society. Some of these Aztec medicinal components prevail. However, with the advent of a predominant approach to health and medicine in Western society, Aztec knowledge and practice is often viewed as inferior or not real.

Medical conditions in pre-Columbian societies were different from those in Europe. As Europeans were attempting to understand discoveries in medicine and to understand illnesses, Mesoamerican natives had created medicinal systems that incorporated herbs and folk treatment. Because of the natives' extensive agricultural and floral knowledge, several of these conditions consisted of symptoms that were successfully treated with herbal medicines. However, some native ailments were not always treated effectively with such treatments and required rituals, massages, or even items of animal origin. An example is a common folk medical syndrome found in contemporary Mexico which was a part of the Aztec Empire. The culture-bound condition, known as *empacho*, is characterized by constipation, usually as a result of eating raw dough; however, this condition can also result from consuming a combination of other types of foods and is often treated with a massage in the back of the patient (Tovar, 2014).

Another common condition that can be traced to pre-Columbian times is *caida de mollera*, or fallen fontanel, which is the sinking of the top part of an infant's head because the skull is not solid within the first months. This condition causes vulnerability in the development of the child's head and brain (Ortiz de Montellano, 1987).

Popular treatments involve a ritualistic practice recorded in some codices and documents dating from pre-Columbian times up to the conquest.

The victim of *caida de mollera* needs to be grabbed from the feet and legs, and the upper part of the head needs to be submerged in warm water to correct the shape of the head of the infant (Ortiz de Montellano, 1987).

This practice can still be found in contemporary Mexico, but other treatments appear to be unique, such as a home remedy that consists of washing the area of the head with soap (Ortiz de Montellano, 1987).

Another culture-bound syndrome in today's Mexican community, which traces back to the Aztec Empire, is called *susto*. This folk medical syndrome is often called "magical fright," or simply "fright." It is a state of shock, with physical and psychological disturbances that result from an extremely shocking event (Trotter II, 1991; Tovar, 2014).

With the arrival of the Spaniards, the medical system established by Hippocrates and later structured by Galen and Avicenna dominated Western society. This system is known as the humoral system and its elements can be seen throughout contemporary Mexico's medical establishment because such a health system was dominant in Spain during the conquest of Mesoamerica. The system was incorporated into the native's new social structure, as were other social structures such as religion and language (Sandler and Chan, 1978).

The humoral system attributes the body's harmony and stability to the relationship and the healthy functioning of four bodily fluids, or humors: blood, phlegm, yellow bile, and black bile. In addition to cold/hot properties, they have wet/dry characteristics that can help in determining the right treatment and proper medications, such as herbs, for illnesses. Different body parts also have similar properties. Therefore, treatment can be conducted with hot/cold and wet/dry characteristics to find the correct homeostasis of the body and eliminate discomfort, disorder, and illness (Rubel, 1964).

Another important element of contemporary Mexico is the role of midwives, known in Spanish as *parteras*. This profession was first seen in ancient Mexico and has persisted in today's society. Because of the solid establishment of Western medicine, people in large cities usually opt to receive prenatal and birthing care in a hospital rather than with a *partera*. These services are still utilized in rural areas, however, and by people with a low socioeconomic status (Kellogg, 1995).

MEXICAN AMERICANS OR AMERICAN MEXICANS

The Americanization of Mexico

After the Spanish conquistadores arrived in Mesoamerica, they gained military control of the region they called New Spain. Together with South

America and other parts of the world, Mexico and what is now Central America became part of the Spanish Empire, and it was not until the early 1800s that different countries began to fight for their independence (Del Castillo and De Leon, 1997). In the case of Mexico, this conflict began in 1810 with the movement initiated by Miguel Hidalgo y Costilla, who is considered the father of the Mexican nation (Del Castillo and De Leon, 1997).

After the fight for independence, social and political disorganization occurred. At that time, the southern U.S. states of California, Arizona, Texas, and New Mexico were also part of Mexico. In 1846, war broke out between the United States and Mexico, disputing the sovereignty of what are now the southern states of the United States The conclusion of the war came after the Treaty of Guadalupe Hidalgo was signed, documenting that Mexico ceded such states to the United States (Del Castillo, 1992).

The Mexican culture within these areas continued to exist even after their transition to a new country (Del Castillo and De Leon, 1997). Several settlers and inhabitants continued to live in these areas and, though part of a new nation, their way of life did not immediately change.

As more Anglo-Americans populated this area, cultural practices began to change. Pressure from the new country to adapt to new requirements, including learning English, started to spread. Numerous examples of discrimination in this regard have persisted into contemporary society. Several authors emphasized Mexican American history, but the work of Américo Paredes focused on maintaining Mexican American folklore, and he exemplified the attitudes of Mexican Americans regarding American white culture (Paredes, 1958, 1993).

One of his best known works is the novel, *With His Pistol in His Hand: A Border Ballad and Its Hero,* published in 1958. Paredes writes about a dispute in 1901 between an Anglo-Texas sheriff and Gregorio Cortez, a Texas Mexican resident of the area. Cortez shoots and kills the sheriff and then flees the authorities. Paredes notes the differences in the legal consequences between the two ethnic and cultural groups represented by the people who had the dispute and points out the Mexican American expressions of pride and identity, even composing and singing a ballad in honor of Cortez (Paredes, 1958).

I had the opportunity to interview Américo Paredes a few months before his death in 1999. He spoke at my high school about his experiences as a scholar from the Rio Grande Valley. He remembered living in Brownsville, Texas in a society dominated by Anglo-Americans and evidently divided between ethnic and cultural backgrounds. He and his peers were not allowed to speak Spanish during class as he moved through middle and high school, and because of this, several of his peers viewed learning to speak English as a way of losing their cultural identity.

MEXICAN AMERICAN RECENT HISTORY

The social descriptions depicted in Paredes' work were a reality for Mexican American communities who suffered from discrimination and prejudice. Because of the proximity and the sharing of cultural practices between the United States and Mexico, particularly in the southern United States, an increase in immigration from Mexico occurred. This movement can still be seen and has caused some controversies and resulted in several social movements, some licit and others not. The topic of contemporary immigration is covered in Chapter 4. However, to fully explain the history of Mexican Americans, it is important to define a movement that promoted immigration to the United States: the Bracero Program.

The Bracero Program

The Bracero Program was an agreement between the Mexican and U.S. governments to encourage Mexican nationals to work in the United States on a temporary basis. The work consisted of agricultural tasks related to the maintenance of the United States railroad system (Rosas, 2011). This agreement was a result of a reported labor shortage in the United States during World War II. Mexican nationals who agreed to participate would receive legal authorization to enter the United States and stay from one to nine months, depending on their work contract (Rosas, 2011). Whenever people did not abide by the rules, their contract was terminated (Rosas, 2011).

Several problems resulted from the Bracero Program. The wages migrant workers received were significantly lower than the wages native workers received doing similar jobs. The migrants worked 10 to 12 hours a day without basic but essential benefits for their well-being, such as health insurance, a place to live, food, or transportation to work, and they lacked the resources to communicate these concerns to the Mexican government (Rosas, 2011). Furthermore, the Bracero Program was available only to men and thus separated families (Rosas, 2011).

Cesar Chavez and Civil Rights

While the Bracero Program was in place from August 6, 1942 until December 31, 1964, employers had the option of hiring Mexican nationals for a lower pay rate. However, when the program was over, the conditions and mistreatment toward workers in agricultural settings continued. Even if the workers were American citizens of Mexican descent, labor conditions were harmful and unfavorable compared with other areas of work and different ethnic groups (Molina, 2011). For example, although the adverse effects of exposure to pesticides for farmworkers were known, employers sprayed pesticides over the produce while farmworkers labored in the field (Rodriguez, 2010–2011).

Because of these abuses, a civil rights movement emerged. In the 1960s, the organization of farmworkers was guided by Cesar Chavez, a Mexican American farmworker who motivated others to request equal rights and humane treatment (Del Castillo and De Leon, 1997).

After the Bracero Program, Cesar Chavez was a crucial figure in creating labor unions, such as today's United Farm Workers of America (Rodriguez, 2010–2011). Among the strategies he and his followers applied were peaceful walkouts and the boycotting of grape harvesting in California (Del Castillo and De Leon, 1997). Because of these union efforts, several changes occurred in labor conditions of farmworkers. In 1975, California passed the California Farm Labor Act but it has undergone several modifications since its establishment, which has led to other movements and boycotts for equal rights and humane work conditions (Del Castillo and De Leon 1997). Achieving significant progress in some areas, labor unions continue to be active in defending the rights of farmworkers (Rodriguez, 2010–2011).

The occurrences of social inequality and discrimination against American citizens of Mexican descent persisted. In the late 1960s and early 1970s, social movements in schools demanded equal rights and respect toward cultural diversity. These movements occurred in different areas of the country, such as California (Del Castillo and De Leon, 1997), and in regions of low socioeconomic status characterized by large Mexican American populations, including the school district of Edcouch-Elsa.

According to students of Mexican descent who attended the district high school in the mid to late 1960s, a predominantly Caucasian administration, staff, and faculty treated students of Mexican descent with a lower educational standard and discriminated against them compared to how Anglo-Americans were treated (Vela, 2014). These discriminatory practices led students to participate in a peaceful walkout from their classrooms and to boycott classes while demanding several conditions be addressed before they returned. The demands included the following:

(1) Excessive and unfair penalties and punishments should stop being given to students for minor infractions, such as a student being suspended for three days for failure to keep an appointment with a teacher after school. (2) Stop the paddling of students for any reason without the students being able to speak and explain themselves. (3) Migrant students should be given tests before leaving to work up north. (4) No teacher or administrator should use profanity. (5) No teacher or

administrator should lay a hand on a student. (6) Students should be allowed to speak their first language (Spanish) without being punished for it. (7) Counselors should be fair and give the same college guidance to Mexican Americans. (8) Teachers and the administration should not practice blatant discrimination. (9) Threats, intimidation, and penalties should stop. (10) Unfairness by teachers and administration should stop. (Vela, 2014)

Although the students were initially expelled and had to attend another high school over 29 miles away, eventually a resolution was found and the students were allowed to return. These types of demonstrations and movements are an important indication of the social characteristics to which some Mexican Americans have been exposed.

SUMMARY

The purpose of this chapter is to cover the history of Mexican Americans, about which many people are unaware. It is important to understand the context and the circumstances that led this population to inhabit the areas in which they currently reside and to understand some of the practices that can be found in today's society. Additionally, understanding some of the difficulties and obstacles Mexican American forefathers had to overcome is important when working with this population, as it provides a clearer and broader picture of what attaining this cultural identity may represent. In Chapter 3, we discuss the characteristics of contemporary Mexican Americans.

Chapter 3

Contemporary Mexican American Society

I was born in the United States and my mother's family primarily resides in South Texas, but I spent many of my formative years in Mexico City. I was aware of cultural practices in South Texas and northern Mexico, but because of the area and the way in which I was raised, I seldom practiced those customs. It was not until I began to socialize more with people from this region that I became aware of several significant differences among people who consider themselves Mexican American; for example, differences between those from the southern and northern parts of Mexico.

A few years ago, I was invited to a party to celebrate the birthday of a friend's grandfather, Pablo. I immediately recognized common elements found in other parties or family reunions in this area: a family member cooking chicken and beef in a barbeque pit with charcoal, and the distinct tone of the music. The bass was very pronounced, and the accordion played solos when the singer did not sing. The songs were about either heroes who fell or dramatic life situations such as the pain of an unfaithful woman. The most interesting part of that night was a long conversation I had with Pablo. He shared several experiences he had as a young man living on the border between Mexico and the United States and dealing with some witches of the region. A particular woman who did not like him much opted to make his life miserable. She put hexes on him for financial hardship and for other difficulties such as arguments with friends and family members. One day, he waited for her outside of her home and followed her without her knowing it. He eventually saw her turn into a *lechuza*, or an owl, and when she saw him from the air she flew toward him with her claws forward as a predator on a hunt after finding its prey. Pablo took a handkerchief from his back pocket and began to make knots as he said some special prayers. After the last knot, the owl turned back into a woman and fell to the ground. After that, the witch lost her powers and left him alone. She left the town and was never heard from again.

The characteristics of contemporary Mexican Americans are very diverse and complex. Therefore, I will give a general overview of some of the most significant social and cultural aspects of this group, covering folklore, food, medicine and ailments, and other contemporary characteristics that assist in better understanding this population.

CHARACTERISTICS OF CONTEMPORARY MEXICAN AMERICANS
Ethnic/Cultural Identification

Several different terms are used to describe a person of Mexican American descent, such as *Chicano, Tejano, Hispanic,* or *Latino* (Shorris, 2012). Although different people may feel more or less comfortable with any of these terms, it is important to recognize the differences among them and be more conscious of what these terms may mean to a person. The term *Latino* refers to "belonging to a certain group of people who are in some fundamental ways related to European Latin countries" (Nuccetelli, 2001; 179). The term *Hispanic* can be defined as "belonging to a certain group of people who are in some fundamental ways related to a former Roman territory located in what is now Spain and Portugal" (Nuccetelli, 2001, p. 179). However, some people consider the word *Hispanics* to describe Spanish-speaking people, particularly those who are in second or later generations, as this can influence the level of acculturation and therefore the learning of the English language (Zimmerman, Vega, Gil, Warheit, Apospori, and Biafora, 1994). In the 1930s, the term *Mexican* was used to describe a race primarily of people born in Mexico whose parents were born in Mexico and who could not be considered part of any other ethnic group (Gibson and Jung, 2002). From the 1940s to the 1970s, there were changes proposed to identify people using other types of characteristics, including primary language and last name (Perez, 2008). Eventually in the early 1980s, the word to describe individuals of Mexican descent changed to Hispanic/Latino (Perez, 2008). The U.S. Census uses the terms *Mexican* or *of Mexican descent,* but these options are offered after a person has been first identified as Hispanic or Latino (Ghazal, 2013).

Another term is *Chicana* or *Chicano*, "A person of Mexican birth or descent residing in the United States (particularly in those areas annexed in 1848), esp. one who is proud of his Mexican origins and concerned to improve the position of Mexicans in the United States; a Mexican American" (*Oxford English Dictionary*, 1989, pp. 104–105). This term has evolved and is used differently from its first use when it described Mexican immigrants who resided in disadvantaged and rural areas (Del Castillo and De Leon, 1997), or as a pejorative term to identify people of Mexican descent residing in the United States (Sánchez-Muñoz, 2013). The emphasis in this definition lies in the place where the person was born. It includes a way of promoting improvement of Mexican Americans within the United States, but does not necessarily include the importance of identification (Jonsson, 2012).

There are other terms that U.S. citizens of Mexican descent may use as a form of identification, depending on the region they are from or where they are residing. The term *chilango* is often used to describe a person from Mexico City (*Merriam-Webster Dictionary Online*), and people may find pride in it as it gives them not only an identity in the United States but also an identity that can be traced to their ancestors or their history before arriving in the United States *Tejano*, which means "a Texan of Mexican descent" (Shorris, 2012; *Webster's New World College Dictionary* 2007, p. 1471), incorporates some elements of the culture of the northern part of Mexico with traits of the Texan culture, creating a new culture known as "Tex-Mex." This new culture includes practices that result from a combination of both Texan and Mexican customs, which can be manifested in food and language, among other social characteristics.

SOCIAL CHARACTERISTICS OF MEXICAN AMERICANS

Music

Corridos   One of the most distinguished types of music forming part of the Mexican American culture, particularly on the border between Mexico and the United States, is what is known as a *corrido*. A *corrido* is a narrative song with lyrics that recount episodes of violent conflict and confrontation (Tatar, 2010). Some authors consider *corridos* to include other topics, such as love, rivalry, and dramatic subjects (Corona Cadena, 2010), while others consider these songs to be ballads that address current political topics and glorify and give tribute to heroes or important events (McDowell, 2012).

Corridos can be described according to three elements of analysis: patronage systems, aesthetics, and dissemination. Patronage systems refer to reciprocal exchanges, such as the troops' request for *corridos* during the Mexican Revolution (McDowell, 2012). The concept of aesthetics refers to the characteristic of the melody (McDowell, 2012). Dissemination refers to the ways in which people are exposed to *corridos*, traditionally through live performances, and more recently, through audio recordings (McDowell, 2012), television, and the Internet.

This music is believed to have migrated from Spain during the conquest (Paredes, 1976) and has adapted to the circumstances surrounding the regions in which it is played and heard. For example, *corridos* were considered a way of communicating news and information regarding the War of the Revolution in Mexico (Paredes, 1976). During social and cultural conflicts between the United States and Mexico, *corridos* became an emblem and a way of sharing information with the general population about the difficulties of immigration or depicting stories about drug lords and their battles against the authorities from both sides of the border (Wald, 2002).

According to some scholars, the music of the *corrido* defines it as much as its lyrics or purpose (Alviso, 2011). The preferred type of instrument in *corridos* is a guitar. Some may involve two guitars, one to play melodies, the other to play chords (Alviso, 2011). These characteristics allow for *corridos* to be easily played anywhere (Alviso, 2011), facilitating the dissemination of news and information throughout society. A harp may substitute for the two guitars, and more than one singer is often involved in the interpretation of the *corrido* (Alviso, 2011).

Narcocorridos   Because of the recent wave of drug trafficking violence in Mexico, a new type of *corrido* sings about the people involved in the drug business and the fight against an established government that is to an extent ineffective in resolving the violence (Corona Cadena, 2010). These *narcocorridos* share elements of other types of *corridos*. *Narcocorridos* are influenced by a large and complex system of networking that includes songwriters, people who perform the songs, and their patrons (McDowell, 2012). They follow the same types of melodies, rhythms, and lyrics as traditional *corridos*, which make them easily identified as songs from this category (McDowell, 2012). And *narcocorridos* follow the same type of dissemination methods as traditional corridos (McDowell, 2012). They face other obstacles, however, such as government censorship (Corona Cadena, 2010).

Soccer

In Mexico, soccer (*futbol*) is a very popular sport. People enjoy playing it and identify with a team in the national league, stopping their daily activities when the game is on television or radio and hoping their team will win. They hope the coach will follow the recommendations of 110 million advisors. This pattern of identity follows that in the United States. It is not surprising to see stadiums full of fans supporting the Mexican national team, even when they play against the United States This behavior denotes a sense of identity that does not necessarily fit into a traditional form of nationalism.

Soccer has been shown to have had a significant impact on athletic activities and is a crucial economic phenomenon that has led people from a low socioeconomic status to practice the game and aspire for a better life (Clark and Burnett, 2010). Practice also can be a sociocultural and ethnic phenomenon that allows individuals to better fit into new and unknown groups. In the case of immigrants, playing and being a fan of soccer can assist in integration into American society in a more effective and complete way. Soccer allows people to seek out other soccer enthusiasts in order to facilitate assimilation and acculturation (Pescador, 2006). Major League Soccer, the U.S. national professional soccer league, has helped promote and encourage the integration of recent immigrants into American society (Pescador, 2004).

In particular regions of the United States, people from different sociocultural and ethnic backgrounds may be motivated to play soccer. In some rural areas with a predominant number of Mexican Americans, it is not uncommon for people to join and play with teams informally, without practice or a coach, because they are close to some of the other players and want to socialize (Pescador, 2004). At the end of some of these games, team members may decide to get together and eat barbeque chicken or grilled meat cooked outside while drinking beer and talking about life.

As with other physical activities, soccer can cause physical injuries. Semiprofessional and professional teams have medical resources and take preventive measures, but these injuries may still significantly impact a person's well-being and future (Rodriguez Gutierrez and Echegoyen Monroy, 2002). Injuries occur in different ways, depending on the player's position in the field and his abilities and history of injuries (Rodriguez Gutierrez and Echegoyen Monroy, 2002). People injured in amateur soccer do not have the resources to pay for treatment and may opt for folk healers or other more economical help, or decide not to seek medical attention, which can affect their everyday lives.

Although soccer is practiced across different locations and socioeconomic groups, implicit rules exist specific to a location. The rules for a professional and amateur soccer game might be the same, but the rewards, incentives, and even motivations are different and demonstrate substantial discrepancies in players' lifestyles on and off the field. People might play soccer to relax and maintain fitness. Others play to socialize and to find people with something in common. Although playing soccer can decrease the risk of developing cardiovascular disease, diabetes, and obesity, it needs to be played with discipline and as part of a more comprehensive health strategy (Leitão Batista, Fernandes Filho, and Silva Dantas, 2007). People who play amateur soccer, particularly those outside of a school setting, tend to get together to play as a cultural practice more than to lose weight or become healthier. These amateurs often play irregularly and do not participate in formal training, leading them to become overweight and risk developing cardiovascular conditions or diabetes (Meireles de Pontes and Cirilo de Sousa, 2009).

Folklore

Like any other cultural group, Mexican American cultural beliefs passed down from generation to generation are assumed to be true or were true at one point. This information, available and transmitted from mouth to ear, provides guidance and allows future generations to learn from previous ones. Some beliefs pertain to knowledge and practices that address ailments and medical conditions; others teach individuals about appropriate social behavior and behaviors that should be avoided to ensure survival and general well-being. In the following section, I will discuss folk medical practices, covered briefly in Chapter 2, more in depth, as well as stories or legends that people generally recognize as true and that dictate behavior according to sociocultural norms.

Folk Medicine   As briefly introduced in Chapter 2, Mexican American folk medicine can be traced to Aztec times and continues to exist in contemporary Mexican and Mexican American societies. After the establishment of New Spain in the region known as Mesoamerica in central Mexico, people began to move north and expanded this territory. They moved away from established hospitals and needed a guide to help them identify and treat ailments. These practices were recorded in documents that were similar to journals and included illustrations. The most famous of these was the *florilegio medicinal* (Tovar, 2014).

When people think of contemporary folk medicine, they commonly think of a *curandero* (a folk healer) or *yerberias* (stores where different herbs are sold for the purpose of folk and magical practices, including healing). However, folk medical practices happen most of the time in regular home environments (Tovar, 2014).

This approach to medicine continues due to several factors. Those who seek out these interventions may not have the financial resources to engage contemporary health care services. A friend or family member can often offer these interventions, which are based on folk knowledge and do not require formal academic education. Furthermore, the interventions are usually things found at home or easily accessible and do not have to be from a pharmacy or require a prescription (Tovar, 2014).

Treatments may require diagnoses or the identification of symptoms known by Western medicine, such as a fever. However, some conditions are specific to this culture and require treatments specific to this form of medicine. The four main types of culture-bound syndromes found in Mexican American culture are *empacho, caida de mollera, mal de ojo,* and *susto* (Tovar, 2014). The first two ailments have more physical and natural properties and are treated as such, whereas the last two have more supernatural and spiritual characteristics.

Empacho is a condition characterized by digestive problems. The person suffering from this condition is believed to have a blockage in the intestines or stomach which is caused by ingestion of a substance such as gum or raw dough (Weller and Baer, 2001; Weller, Pachter, Trotter II, and Baer, 1993), swallowing too much saliva, eating food that was not fully cooked, or eating too much food (Weller *et al.*, 1993). People who eat too late or too early in the day may also suffer from this condition (Weller *et al.*, 1993). Symptoms may go beyond constipation to diarrhea and vomiting, inflammation of the stomach, indigestion, and general body weakness (Weller *et al.*, 1993).

The treatment for *empacho* can include drinking teas and substances that allow the person suffering from it to purge (Trotter II and Chavira, 1997), or receiving a specialized massage of the stomach (Trotter II, 1991) or of the back, pulling the skin from the back until it "pops" (Trotter II and Chavira, 1997).

Caida de mollera, or fallen fontanelle, is another folk medical condition characteristic of Mexican American culture. It is only found in infants and is characterized by the sinking of the top part of an infant's skull, or fontanelle (Baer and Bustillo, 1998). *Caida de mollera* can also cause fever, a decreased appetite, and diarrhea (Baer and Bustillo, 1998). This condition is believed to result from an infant receiving a blow to the head or being shaken, or if the bottle or breast is detached too suddenly from the mouth while the child is eating (Baer and Bustillo, 1998). The most common treatments for this condition include holding the child upside down by the ankles and slightly hitting the soles of the feet until the fontanelle returns to its original position, submerging the fontanelle in water while holding the child upside down, or pushing the upper part of the mouth, or palate, up (Ortiz de Montellano, 1987).

Mal de ojo and *susto* are two of the best known conditions in the Mexican American population. They have unique properties, as both are personalistic conditions but they share similarities related to supernatural characteristics of their conditions and treatments (Tovar, 2014).

Mal de ojo can be translated literally as "evil eye." However, the condition does not necessarily involve evil intentions or the desire to cause harm. The condition can cause a person to become sick or can cause an item to break or stop working after someone admires the person or the item. The admirer does not necessarily want to cause any harm or feel envious. After exposure, the victim may suffer flu-like symptoms such as headaches, fever, or stomach problems such as diarrhea (Tovar, 2014; Baer and Bustillo, 1993).

Children are particularly vulnerable, as adults often admire them. Toddlers may suffer symptoms similar to adults, but infants may show general discomfort and cry constantly without apparent reason. If someone touches the person or item right after the admiration, it is believed the condition can be prevented. Another preventative measure is the use of *ojo de venado*, or deer's eye. This is a seed that is worn as a necklace or bracelet, believed to absorb the energy that causes this condition. The absorption results in the destruction of the seed (Tovar, 2014).

If preventive methods are not effective, several other remedies may alleviate the condition. The most common is a ritual known as a *barrida*, or sweeping, using a raw egg to "sweep" the person's body, sometimes in small crosses, while saying prayers such as the "Our Father." The egg is then opened and poured into a full glass of water. If it absorbed the energy or "evil" responsible for the symptoms, the egg will have a darker appearance and is considered to be "cooked" (Baer and Bustillo, 1993).

A similar ritual used to treat *mal de ojo* is conducted with a type of rock called a *piedra lumbre*. In this procedure, instead of putting the rock inside a glass of water, it is put on a griddle or a hot pan. The heat cracks the stone, shaping it to take the form of the cause of the condition. The rock often takes the shape of the face of the admirer who caused the ailment. Sometimes, the ritual is also performed with herbs. Although it is not required, some people grow their own plants for sweeping or for making a tea that will calm the symptoms (Trotter II and Chavira, 1997).

Susto can be literally translated as fright, but this condition involves a more complex definition and origin. In the folk medical realm, this condition is considered to be magical fright caused when a person is exposed to a frightening or traumatic experience. The person usually begins to feel more anxious than usual, has some difficulties sleeping and eating, and suffers from frequent headaches, nausea, and vomiting (Castro and Eroza, 1998).

Because of such symptoms, *susto* can be mistaken for other types of Western medical conditions such as post-traumatic stress disorder, or PTSD

(Logan, 1993). In some cases of *susto* the onset of the illness may denote symptoms found in depression and anxiety (Logan, 1993). Unlike *mal de ojo, susto* cannot be prevented once the person is exposed to the frightening or traumatic experience.

Treatments include natural substances or supernatural rituals. One of the most common treatments is a spoonful of sugar right after experiencing a traumatic or frightening situation. In some cases, a healer may choose to dispense salt or a piece of bread. Although healers do not have clinical, biological, or chemical justifications for their treatments, researchers suggest that after a person undergoes a frightening event, he or she may experience a hypoglycemic episode, which explains the person's relief in consuming sugar or in eating bread (Tovar, 2014).

Rituals to alleviate symptoms of *susto* contain supernatural elements and are often used when it is believed the soul or part of the soul of the person has left the body after being exposed to the frightening event. One of these rituals consists of saying prayers at the location of the frightening event while asking for the soul of the person to return to the body (Trotter II and Chavira, 1997).

Another ritual places the victim of this condition face down in a cross-shaped position. The healer performs a sweeping with herbs and says prayers asking for the soul to return to the body (Trotter II and Chavira, 1997). The primary purpose of these rituals is to recover the lost soul as soon as possible. If the remedy is not applied in time, the lost soul may not be recovered, and the body may leave an empty space that can be occupied by another soul (Tousignant, 1982). Not everyone who believes in *susto* thinks the soul leaves the body. Some believe that what is lost when the person experiences a frightening or traumatic event is a "vital force" (Glazer, Baer, Weller, Garcia de Alba, and Liebowitz, 2004).

A survey to obtain comparative information about different folk medical syndromes revealed considerable differences in the frequency of the treatments between male subjects (13.7 percent) and female subjects (86.3 percent) interviewed. The two folk medical syndromes treated with more frequency historically were *susto* (62.4 percent) and *mal de ojo* (63.1 percent). They had the highest prevalence of being treated during the 12 months before the survey was conducted, at 27.1 percent and 20.4 percent, respectively (Trotter II, 1991)

Urban/Contemporary Legends

Mexican American culture's urban or contemporary legends dictate social rules, prescriptions, and proscriptions. Like other urban legends, they are characterized by having no clear origin and are usually transmitted by those who believe them to be true. Two of the most popular urban legends in the Mexican American population are *La Llorona* and *The Devil at the Disco*.

La Llorona   This contemporary legend has its roots in Mexico. Depending on the region where it is heard, some circumstances and characteristics may change to fit into the characteristics of the area where it is told. In different regions of the United States, this story has changed as well, but the common elements are not different. The story is about a mother of three who has marital problems. On one occasion, the woman gets into an argument with her husband who decides to leave her. The woman then kills her children and then kills herself. It is believed that her spirit wanders the streets crying for her children. The word *llorona* refers to a woman who cries.

Some variations of this story include details about the type of conflict the woman had with her husband (whether he leaves her for another woman or just leaves her), the psychosocial problems she may have experienced (in some stories the family is of a low socioeconomic status), and the method used to kill her children (by stabbing, or in areas where there are canals or rivers, by drowning). A version of this story from Mexico takes place during the colonization of Mesoamerica. In this version, the woman is native indigenous, and the man is a Spaniard.

Devil at the Disco   This story can be found in several cultures. Just as with *La Llorona,* the content has similar elements across different versions which permits this story to be easily recognized. The version found in the Mexican American population contains characteristics that dictate social and cultural norms found in Mexican American culture. The story usually begins with a young woman going to a local dance even though her parents had prohibited her from going. She meets an elegant man who asks her to dance. They dance until midnight, when the woman realizes the man has a hoof for a foot. They start to spin around while levitating together. Once they reach the roof, the man disappears, and the woman falls to the ground, dead.

SOCIAL PERCEPTIONS AND ATTITUDES WITHIN CONTEMPORARY MEXICAN AMERICAN SOCIETY

In addition to social characteristics of the Mexican American population, specific characteristics exist of social interactions within the group. In this section, we will cover the concepts of *machismo, marianismo,* and *familismo.*

Machismo refers to the ideas, behaviors, and feelings that denote dominance in a person's relationships by implying and showing superiority over others (Marrs Fuchsel, Murphy, and Dufresne, 2012). Some authors consider *machismo* to contain both positive and negative elements. Positive machismo refers to committing to one's own beliefs, gaining respect from other people, and maintaining family as the most important part of a person's life (Pardo, Weisfeld, Hill, and Slatcher, 2013). Negative machismo reflects the domineering aspect of the concept, including the imposition and control of family to demonstrate masculine characteristics, sometimes resulting in aggressive acts and violence (Pardo *et al.*, 2013).

Marianismo is used to describe how women are expected to behave (Piña-Watson, Castillo, and Castillo-Reyes, 2014). These characteristics of behavior include interdependence, a higher level of spirituality than men, a sense of altruism, purity, and submissiveness, and sacrificing for the benefit of the family (Piña-Watson, Castillo, and Castillo-Reyes, 2014). *Marianismo* is believed to emerge from three major principles: *simpatía, respeto, and familismo*. *Simpatía* refers to "the expectation that one maintains harmony in relationships through smooth and pleasant interactions" (Piña-Watson *et al.*, 2014). *Respeto*, or respect, includes the ability and willingness to be obedient, to do one's own duty, and to accept one's place within a social hierarchy (Piña-Watson *et al.*, 2014).

Familismo

In Mexican American society, just as in other Hispanic or Latino groups, the relationship with a person's own family is crucial to the person's general well-being. The term *familismo* describes the closeness a person may have to his or her family (Sotomayor-Peterson, Figueredo, Christensen, and Taylor, 2012). An important part of this concept is loyalty and connections with different family members, something that results from having the concept of the family as a central element of the person's life (Piña-Watson, Ojeda, Castellon, and Dornhecker, 2013).

WELL-BEING OF MEXICAN AMERICANS

In recent years, several types of health conditions have increasingly affected the Mexican American population. Although the prevalence of some of these conditions in Mexican Americans has existed for some time, the presence of others, and the number of people within this group who suffer such conditions, have increased considerably. Several scholars have attempted to explain why this phenomenon has occurred. Some believe that the level of acculturation and assimilation plays a role in the development of health conditions and the general deterioration of one's well-being, which we will cover more in depth in Chapter 5. Possible causes may be as varied and diverse as subgroups within the Mexican American population. In this section, we will cover some of the most common conditions that have affected the Mexican American population and that are responsible for a very high number of deaths within this group.

Diabetes

A few years ago, while working at a community mental health agency, I had a conversation with a newly employed nurse about the prevalence of diabetes in communities along the border of Mexico and the United States. He said if a clinical team of a hospital is unable to determine whether a person suffers from diabetes, the team commonly assumes so due to the high incidences of this condition in the region and group. Diabetes is a health care problem across the nation, but Latinos are about 66 percent more likely to be diagnosed with it compared with non-Latino whites (Hanni, Ahn, and Winkleby, 2013). Mexican Americans are at an 87 percent higher risk compared to non-Latino whites (Hanni et al., 2013). It is believed that cultural beliefs, socioeconomic status, access to health care, and lifestyle play a role in the development of this condition (Vincent, 2009).

Obesity plays an important role in the development of different conditions and increases the risk of diabetes, even at an early age. A relationship exists between maternal body mass index and child weight: mothers who fall into the clinical category of obesity are more likely to have children who are overweight or obese (Morello, Madanat, Crespo, Lemus, and Elder, 2012). More Mexican American youth have been diagnosed with diabetes (May and Rew, 2009), and an increased number of adolescents meet the clinical criteria for obesity or are overweight (May and Rew, 2009). This condition is likely due to a lack of exercise and an inadequate diet (May and Rew, 2009). Obesity and being overweight can lead to other health conditions that form part of what is known as metabolic syndrome, such as high cholesterol and increased body mass index.

Heart Disease

Cardiovascular disease refers to ailments of the blood vessels and heart. Heart disease refers only to conditions that directly affect the heart. Diabetes increases the risk of developing conditions such as blockages of the arteries and heart disease (Vijayaraghavan, He, Stoddard, and Schillinger, 2010). Studies have found risk factors for heart disease such as elevated total and LDL levels of cholesterol, high blood pressure, smoking, and even diabetes. The Mexican American population is vulnerable to the development of these conditions (Morales, Leng, and Escarce, 2011).

Some studies provide information about prevention and management of these conditions (Schlomann, Hesler, Fister, and Taft, 2012). Physical activity and a healthy balanced diet can help reduce risk. In the Mexican American population, accurate perceptions about the importance of a healthy diet and regular physical exercise can contribute to the general improvement of the population's well-being, particularly in the case of immigrants (Schlomann *et al.*, 2012).

SUMMARY

In this chapter, we discuss the contemporary characteristics of Mexican Americans. Some of the content pertains to history, such as folkloric health practices, but the fact that these practices continue to be an important part of Mexican American society makes the content important to people who work with this population in a variety of roles. Although important concepts and topics are covered in this chapter, the information required to describe contemporary Mexican Americans requires more space than a single chapter. In the following chapters, we discuss in greater detail topics that characterize the Mexican American population, such as immigration, the role of acculturation and assimilation, and language.

Chapter 4

Undocumented Immigration and Mexican Americans

A couple of weeks before I finished this chapter, Donald Trump announced that he aspired to become the Republican candidate for the 2016 U.S. presidential election, making several remarks during his announcement about Mexican immigrants. People from different ethnic and cultural groups openly expressed their discontent with the inaccuracy and discriminatory nature of such statements, which could elicit hatred and prejudice. Specifically, Trump stated: "When Mexico sends its people, they're not sending their best. . . . They're bringing drugs. They're bringing crime. They're rapists . . . and some, I assume, are good people." These remarks demonstrate the rhetoric here in recent years regarding immigration to the United States. This topic has been covered in great detail by the media and adopted by politicians, activists, and others who have the opportunity of speaking to the masses, and it has resulted in a diverse set of opinions.

Some people are in favor of immigration but not of illegal immigration, and they think every undocumented individual in the United States should return to his or her place of origin. Others support providing legal status to over 11 million undocumented immigrants and also support making the borders more secure. A major obstacle that influences opinion about this topic is the available information people have regarding immigrants, and sometimes that information is lacking or greatly misunderstood and distorted by a mindset of fear. This chapter presents scholarly information about this topic, aiming to clarify truths and remove myths regarding immigration and immigrants.

DISCRIMINATION

The United States is a constantly changing society. Its economy attracts immigrants from all over the world, making it a multicultural country. With so many different groups residing in the United States, several customs and practices may be unknown, sometimes creating hostilities. Discrimination and prejudice can occur both consciously and unconsciously, and it is present in every society at one time or another.

Hispanics and Mexican Americans have been exposed to negative attitudes not only because of the color of their skin, but also because of their language and cultural practices, which differ from other groups.

Organizations have been formed to protest the discrimination these groups have experienced and to defend their rights, especially for people of low socioeconomic status who often are unable to speak English or to defend themselves (Romero, 2005).

Some people do not know how to react to acts of discrimination and racism and learn to cope with such negative attitudes as if they were normal. Some conclude that nothing can be done to change them, and they develop a level of helplessness as discrimination occurs routinely at work, in school, in stores, and even in church (Vasquez, 2005).

Hispanics and Mexican Americans constantly face circumstances that can create social prejudice. Although they are one of the fastest growing minority groups, they face a notorious lack of social services available to them to help them, and they face challenges to the delivery of such services, such as a language barrier. In marketing, this population is consciously included in advertising campaigns. Yet, social services have not reached that point (Suleiman, 2003).

Hispanics and Mexican Americans with low levels of education who speak Spanish as their first language and have lower socioeconomic status tend to be particularly vulnerable to discrimination (Wilson, 2007).

In recent years, Mexican Americans have experienced increased opportunities to better themselves, their well-being, and their lifestyle. However, there remain discrepancies in opportunities compared to their white Caucasian counterparts. For example, although Mexican Americans are more likely to attend college or university than ever before, they still do not have as many opportunities to attend universities with high academic prestige (Trillo, 2004).

It is common for people to get together with others who share the same interests. This social phenomenon can promote negative attitudes toward certain groups. In a study conducted by McGlothlin and Killen (2006), evidence shows European-American children who shared a classroom with other children from their own ethnicity had a tendency to show more negative attitudes toward people from different ethnicities than children who shared a classroom with children from different ethnic groups.

MEXICAN IMMIGRANTS

Because of Mexico's proximity with the United States, Mexicans form the majority of immigrants in the United States. It is estimated that of 11.6 million undocumented immigrants, 60 percent are of Mexican descent (Diaz, Saenz, and Kwan, 2011). Several social, political, and economic changes throughout the years have influenced people from Mexico and other countries to move to the United States to improve their way of life and to seek well-being for their family. Immigration from Mexico was not always condemned. On the contrary, just as in the case of the Bracero Program (see Chapter 2), it was promoted and facilitated by the United States government to address the country's needs, usually economic needs.

The topic of immigration has taken different paths, and the social and political context that surrounds it has evolved. Nevertheless, some characteristics have remained the same. The Bracero Program served to attract young males. Because the work that Mexican immigrants were invited to do was primarily in agricultural settings, the people who participated in it were from rural areas (Del Castillo and De Leon, 1997). This situation has not changed much from the characteristics of contemporary immigrants. Most of today's Mexican immigrants are males from rural areas (Kaestner and Malamud, 2014). The number of Mexican immigrants to the United States has also increased in the past decade, placing this population at one-third of all United States residents who were not born in this country (Kaestner and Malamud, 2014). However, recent research suggests Mexican immigration has decreased since the year 2000 (Rios Contreras, 2014). Mexican immigrants also began to expand and populate new areas, particularly since the 1980s, and have gradually increased over the following years (Johnston, Karageorgis, and Light, 2013). The reasons for this change include political changes in traditional areas, which pushed immigrants to other areas. For example, in 1994, Proposition 187 in California restricted health care and academic services for undocumented immigrants. As a result, other United States destinations began to be attractive to immigrants, such as Arizona, Georgia, Pennsylvania, and Missouri (Massey and Capoferro, 2008).

One question scholars, politicians, and activists ask is why Mexican nationals may prefer to come to the United States as undocumented rather than through the legal means available to them. One answer may be that the process to enter the United States is complex and, for some people, extremely difficult (Moya Salas, Ayón, and Gurrola, 2013). Some of these processes have been set up to restrict legal admission to the United States of criminals and others who would cause havoc and problems. However, the vast majority of people attempting to come to this country are hardworking people who simply want a better life for themselves and their families (Chalfin, 2014).

Anti-Immigrant Sentiment

In contemporary politics, the topic of immigration has helped distinguish different ideologies. Conservatives tend to favor stricter immigration policies, including building a wall on the border, tightening restrictions on permission to enter the country, and implementing rules to ensure the deportation of undocumented immigrants, regardless of their status or contributions to society. Liberals, on the other hand, tend to favor assistance for undocumented immigrants, including help in receiving a higher education, and a pathway toward citizenship and legalization of those already in this country as undocumented migrants.

These ideologies are magnified by a divided media. Whereas networks like FOX News support conservative views of immigration, MSNBC or CNN tend to favor more liberal ideas (Gil de Zúñiga, Correa, and Valenzuela, 2012). The general population decides which network to follow based on their predisposed ideology, but the sentiment of these networks tends to influence the audience. Particularly in the case of FOX News, which studies suggest strongly supports conservative views (Gil de Zúñiga *et al.*, 2012), it is not uncommon to hear negative views about undocumented immigrants.

In 2010, Arizona launched Senate Bill 1070, making it legal to profile people of Latino or Hispanic origin, regardless of their migratory status (Toomey, Umaña-Taylor, Williams, Harvey-Mendoza, Jahromi, and Updegraff, 2014). This bill has led to several social issues in the community, including the amplifying of people's fear of seeking out needed services. For example, adolescent mothers of Mexican descent were not as likely to seek medical assistance for their infant due to fear of this immigration law (Toomey *et al.*, 2014). These mothers were also less likely to pursue preventive medical services, even though they are a high-risk population (Toomey *et al.*, 2014).

Perceptions like those portrayed by conservative media and laws like the one proposed in Arizona lead immigrants to live in constant fear and even to develop trauma (Moya Salas, Ayón, and Gurrola, 2013). Undocumented immigrants may feel no control or power in their daily lives and may develop an ongoing state of distress (Moya Salas *et al.*, 2013).

On the border with Mexico, armed groups have attempted to detain undocumented people who cross the border. These groups are not part of a law enforcement entity; they are concerned with the inability of authorities to address the issue and have decided to take action themselves (Moya Salas *et al.*, 2013). These groups also contribute to the level of anxiety in immigrant families, which can have repercussions in various areas of the United States (Moya Salas *et al.*, 2013). One example is at the Arizona border. This group, self-identified as "minutemen," conducts raids to arrest undocumented individuals (Moya Salas *et al.*, 2013).

Whenever undocumented immigrants are detained and deported, social problems arise, starting with the immediate family members and extending to the areas in which the deported individual contributed. Research suggests about 60 percent of Latinos in the United States have concerns a friend, a family member, or even they themselves will be deported (Moya Salas *et al.*, 2013), including children who may be U.S. citizens (Chaudry, Capps, Pedroza, Castañeda, Santos, and Scott, 2010).

In addition to media influence, some social scientists believe a main reason for anti-immigrant sentiment is fear of competition. Several instances in the history of this country have shown that economic competition elicited negative perceptions toward another group (Diaz *et al.*, 2011). A person with similar characteristics to those found in immigrants would be more likely to react negatively toward immigrants than those who have no reason to feel threatened by their arrival. This fear of competition can also explain why some Mexican Americans oppose immigrants, regardless of the fact that they share a similar cultural context.

From 2006 to 2009, an increased negative perception had occurred about undocumented immigration from Mexico (Diaz *et al.*, 2011). This increase seemed to have been directly correlated to decreased employment opportunities in the United States (Diaz *et al.*, 2011). Although some Latinos have expressed negative attitudes toward undocumented immigration, the perceptions of European Americans are generally more negative than other cultural groups (Diaz *et al.*, 2011). Middle-aged and older Mexican Americans are believed to have more negative perceptions than younger generations, possibly because the younger generations have had more opportunities to develop into a different social area with greater exposure to multiculturalism than older generations, which witnessed several social and political actions opposing different groups (Jiménez, 2009).

VIOLENCE, MENTAL HEALTH, AND IMMIGRATION

As with the comments made by Donald Trump, there have been several instances where politicians and others have suggested that Mexican immigrants only contribute negatively to the United States. Violence and mental health issues are two topics associated with undocumented immigrants. Research suggests that people who are less acculturated to U.S. society are less likely to suffer from mental illness. In contrast, immigrants who are more acculturated are more likely to suffer from mental illness (Albraído-Lanza, Chao, and Flórez, 2005). This issue is discussed more in depth in Chapter 5.

Shortly after Donald Trump's unfortunate comments, an undocumented immigrant was responsible for the death of a woman in San Francisco, CA. Because the man had been deported five times, those who favored Trump's comments used the case to associate violence and crime with Mexican immigration, and research suggests that public opinion aligned with this association (Espenshade and Hempstead, 1996). Mexican immigration, however, has not been shown to contribute to increases in U.S. crime rates (Chalfin, 2014), and Mexican immigrants are less likely to engage in any type of violence (Borges, Rafful, Tancredi, Saito, Aguilar-Gaxiola, Medina-Mora, and Breslau, 2013).

Mexican immigrants are at a higher risk of being victims of sexual violence and other acts, such as kidnapping or hostage taking (Borges *et al.*, 2013). People who, in addition to being migrants, suffer from a mental illness are more likely to be victims of violence (Borges *et al.*, 2013). Once these migrants arrive in the United States, they may not have the resources to cope with the conflicts that result from such trauma or abuse.

VIOLENCE IN MEXICO

The total number of Mexican nationals migrating to the United States has decreased constantly since 2000, but the cities located across the border between these two countries have experienced the opposite. A main reason for this population growth is violence in the northern states of Mexico related to disputes within organized crime (Rios Contreras, 2014). This situation has also led to a decline in U.S. citizens traveling to the border towns of Mexico (Ramirez III, Argueta, and Grasso, 2013).

U.S. ECONOMY AND UNDOCUMENTED IMMIGRANTS

Concerns about immigrants negatively affecting the U.S. economy have been expressed. Some people have reported that immigrants take jobs away from permanent residents or U.S. citizens. Others think their tax dollars are supporting undocumented immigrants who are using U.S. resources. Research suggests these perceptions are inaccurate, and, on the contrary, immigrants' impact on the U.S. economy can be more positive than negative.

Undocumented immigrants tend to have lower wages than documented U.S. workers (Chalfin, 2014), and their tax contributions have been shown to benefit the American economy (Porter, 2005). Furthermore, their specific labor is essential for some industries to work efficiently. For example, a few years ago, because of the recent anti-immigration sentiment and rhetoric, a decline in Mexican immigration to the United States led many businesses that rely on their work, such as agriculture, to struggle. Documented immigrants, for example, were not able to perform fruit picker jobs correctly or were not interested in these jobs, and fruit eventually rotted in the fields, costing the industry a considerable amount of money

Some ask why this anti-immigrant sentiment and attitude exists. Why select this group of people to attack? Manipulation of opinions by the media and a general misconception about this group facilitates xenophobia. Perhaps understanding the process and experiences immigrants go through to reach a better life can help in humanizing the situation.

The Path to Reach the United States and the Adaptation Process

To understand this complex topic, we need to clarify a few things. First, Mexico is a very diverse country, and people from different parts of Mexico may have different experiences when coming to the United States. Immigrants from Mexican border towns may share several social and cultural characteristics with U.S. border towns, as in the examples of South Texas and the northern part of Tamaulipas. Most of these areas are rural and are constant witnesses to migrants coming and going. Due to shared characteristics and proximity to the United States, residents of the northern states of Mexico may be more familiar with the process of crossing to the southern United States. However, violence from organized crime has recently increased.

The process for people traveling from other parts of Mexico to the northern parts of the United States may be more complicated. One of the advantages of traveling to the border towns is that, in addition to common sociocultural practices, a larger number of people speak Spanish.

One of the most common criticisms against undocumented immigrants is that they should only obtain access to the United States through the established processes. But the process can be very lengthy and require resources individuals may not have in their country of origin. Furthermore, several steps in the process were created so U.S. officials could exclude qualified people. This process may have blocked people who could bring harm to the United States, but it has also excluded people who may contribute to the growth of this country, usually because of a lack of resources here. Another important factor to consider is that a number of undocumented immigrants residing in the United States (not only of Mexican descent but from other countries) arrived through legal means, but failed to renew their documentation or exited the country when they were supposed to (Warren and Kerwin, 2015).

Language can play a role in the successful adaptation, assimilation, and eventual acculturation of immigrants to U.S. society. Those who do not speak English or are unable to communicate in English can be prevented from personally developing and moving up the social ladder. The fact that Spanish is the second most commonly spoken language in the United States facilitates basic human activities, such as shopping.

Research has shown that parental involvement can play an important role in reducing the risk of children seeking drugs and engaging in risky sexual behaviors. They are more likely to complete high school and obtain higher grades (Behnke, Taylor, and Parra-Cardona, 2008).

Without a doubt, immigration affects and may even change social and cultural practices, and parenting is no exception. The differences in the general ideology and social perception of the United States from the ideology of the country of origin can play a role.

The culture in Mexico is predominately collectivistic, unlike the individualistic ideology of the United States. Traditional Mexican families consider the father and husband to be solely responsible for financially supporting the family. Because of social characteristics in the United States, more egalitarian roles exist within families. Even if the father does not completely adopt to this situation right away, the constant exposure to it promotes and encourages a change in family relationships (Behnke *et al.*, 2008).

Another factor that can contribute to these sociocultural changes is the opportunities available to women. Women of Mexican descent who reside in the United States tend to be more actively employed than women in Mexico (King, 2011).

Legal versus Illegal versus Undocumented Immigrants

Mexican immigrants are classified in several ways. Unfortunately, some people tend to generalize this group and are not sensitive enough to detect differences that can say a lot about a person's possible stressors and social perceptions. The tone of political speech regarding immigration, such as proposed legislation, directly affects undocumented immigrants as well as Mexican Americans who have been in this country, some even for many generations. Laws and policies encourage profiling or identifying individuals suspected of being undocumented based on the color of their skin, their accent, and their social and cultural characteristics (Toomey *et al.*, 2014; Diaz *et al.*, 2011).

From Undocumented to Illegal

While teaching numerous college courses over several years in towns near the Mexican border, I have had conversations with students about the words *undocumented* and *illegal* to describe people who do not have documents to legally reside in the United States. Over the years, I have found that the term *illegal* has become the norm, and people aren't thinking of the consequences of using this term.

The term *illegal immigrant* is often used to describe an individual who entered the United States on an undocumented status. Like many other issues in society, the process of coming to the United States without any documents and through nonstandard, nonestablished means cannot be simply summarized with a single term. Several people who use the term *illegal* do so because undocumented immigrants came to the United States without legal documents and are therefore breaking the law. The term, however, is not used with all people who break laws, including those not following the speed limit. The term *illegal* devalues a specific type of individual, creating discontent and in some cases abhorrence that leads to discrimination and racism (Sarabia, 2012).

Some scholars believe the concept of an individual who is *illegal* was created by political decisions and laws that changed the way people view undocumented immigrants.

Before 1965, there was no limit to the number of people who could enter the United States. The Immigration and Nationality Act of 1965 limited the number of immigrants from countries from the Western Hemisphere (Sarabia, 2012). These limitations were the first of many that led people to seek alternative ways into the United States. Unfortunately, these limitations also have created a culture of rejection and have caused these immigrants to be labeled *illegal*.

The Immigration Reform and Control Act of 1986 was divided into three sections: bringing sanctions to employers who hired undocumented individuals; facilitating the process for people already in the United States to obtain documents and legal status; and creating a program that permitted people who worked in agricultural settings to apply for legalization and also allowing new workers into the United States if an increased need existed for them (Sarabia, 2012). With this reform came an increase in Border Patrol funding (Sarabia, 2012), which eventually led to the border being "militarized" (Gentsch and Massey, 2011). This Act was beneficial for several undocumented immigrants already in the United States, but others did not qualify, and increased funding for the Border Patrol created more hostility toward undocumented immigrants who came later to the United States (Sarabia, 2012). Furthermore, these actions did little to implement new ways to request access to the United States through legal means.

The Illegal Immigration Reform and Immigration Responsibility Act of 1996 continued to criminalize undocumented immigrants. It included a thorough description of the deportation process and set new rules that kept certain individuals from re-entering the country. Additionally, it allowed for some people to be deported without a judicial review (Sarabia, 2012).

It is important to mention that some undocumented immigrants come to the United States and commit serious crimes. Information about the way the undocumented immigrant has been criminalized is not to exclude every person, but to explain that the vast majority of undocumented immigrants come to this country to contribute to the economy and to its general social well-being. To understand the severity of the laws and the problems created with an irrefutable decision using current penalizations, consider the following case:

Jorge, a 55-year-old undocumented Mexican immigrant originally from Matamoros, Tamaulipas, came to the United States in the year 2000. He has worked as a carpenter for a construction company since he arrived.

Prior to coming to the United States as an undocumented immigrant, he attempted to follow the process through legal means. However, he was denied permission because he did not have the profile to contribute to United States society. He and his wife had five children ages 12, 11, 8, 7, and 4. His wife cleaned houses and washed other people's clothes, and together they earned enough money to cover their basic necessities, such as clothing, food, water, and the monthly rent for a small apartment. However, Jorge was left without a job when his employer moved to another part of the country. After five months of struggling, he decided to come to Texas, where a friend promised him a job as a carpenter assistant.

Jorge hired a "coyote," a person who assists in crossing people over the border. He worked in the United States as a carpenter, earning less than half of the minimum wage and without health insurance or other assistance. He started working eight hours a day, but began working up to 16 when he was offered additional hours for the same rate. After working there five years, he was able to buy an old car and bring his family to the United States, where his children immediately started attending school. Jorge's wife began to take English classes at a community center, and they all lived in a small one-bedroom apartment.

On one evening, after work, Jorge was stopped at a random checkpoint established by the sheriff's department in conjunction with the Border Patrol. Such stations were in place to stop people who had pending charges or delinquent traffic tickets, but they also were identifying and detaining people who did not have documents to reside in the United States

Because Jorge did not have documents, he was arrested and taken to a detention center where he was held until he was scheduled for a hearing before a federal judge. The judge determined he would be deported and could not enter the country by any means for five years. Failure to abide by this sanction would result in criminal charges and jail time. He was taken to the nearest border town in Mexico, though he was not from there. He contacted family members still residing in Mexico and stayed with them while his wife and five children continued to live in the United States without any source of income, and without a husband and father.

There are thousands of people experiencing similar circumstances on a daily basis. The laws are very clear; however, they do not consider every possible circumstance or the consequences toward the people affected by such sanctions. In this case, Jorge was not a harmful person and came to the United States just to support his family and to offer them a better future than they were likely to achieve in Mexico. The social consequences of these sanctions may be more harmful than positive for U.S. society. For example, if Jorge is not there to provide for his family, the oldest children may have to drop out of school to provide financial support for the family. Now consider another variable that commonly occurs in cases of deportation: What if the children are American citizens and their parents are not? What kind of negative impact can the deportation of parents have on the children?

Exclude for a moment that Jorge did not have documents to legally reside in the United States and consider that this person as a human being. Is this humane or productive for any family?

SUMMARY

This chapter presents information about immigration and its role in the lives of many Mexican Americans. Mexican immigrants may suffer from discrimination. They are accused of being criminals and are blamed for many social problems they are not a part of. Some information about economics and violence is presented in this chapter to clarify some of this misinformation and to show that the majority of immigrants contribute to society in a positive way. By understanding the impact of immigration on Mexican Americans, it is possible to be sensitive to the needs of such clients receiving mental health services. The following chapter focuses on acculturation and assimilation processes of Mexican Americans.

Chapter 5

Assimilation and Acculturation of Mexican Americans

Two United States towns played a big role in my development as a person and in my profession. The towns of Edcouch and Elsa are small compared with other regions of this nation. They are located in South Texas, very close to the Mexican border, and are considered primarily rural. Their populations largely consist of seasonal migrant workers, which implies that during the summer, workers relocate to northern states where they work in agricultural fields. The towns share a high school, which is located between them, and the towns' populations are predominantly Mexican American. As I started high school, I realized that there was another variable to add to the equation: The Mexican Americans were very diverse. A lot of the students were second- or third-generation Mexican Americans; however, some had just arrived to the United States and only spoke Spanish. Their customs and traditions did not differ much from the practices in the area. Though they had come from another country and did not speak the language, they identified with the culture of the border, as some were from towns just 20 minutes away. The food was the same as in the northern part of Mexico, and the music was very similar, as was the weather.

The difficulty for me was adapting to such characteristics. The customs that some Mexican citizens considered to be normal were foreign to me, having come from Mexico City. I was not used to the music or the food or the heat in South Texas. So many years later, people still ask me if I have gotten used to these characteristics. I have adopted most of the culture as my own. However, it took some time.

Throughout this chapter, we will talk about the assimilation and acculturation that Mexican Americans go through. I first cover Berry's theory of acculturation to explain acculturation stages and processes. Then I cover the relationship between acculturation and mental health, followed by a general description of social relationships and health factors as part of the acculturation process. Last, I review a variety of standard and formal methods to evaluate acculturation.

OVERVIEW OF ACCULTURATION

The first definitions of acculturation were usually based on theories from anthropology. However, some psychologists interested in both psychological and cultural processes decided to create a more complex definition that permits the incorporation of both areas of study (Sam and Berry, 2010). Acculturation can be defined as the psychological and behavioral change resulting from the contact and interaction of two cultures (Sam and Berry, 2010). Acculturation psychology is defined as changes in psychological processes people experience when they meet a different culture (Graves, 1967).

A person's level of acculturation influences his or her's daily life. Those who are able to function in activities within their own culture, such as working, may be affected by levels of acculturation (Osuna and Navarro, 2008). Levels of acculturation may influence the use of community resources (Berdahl and Torres Stone, 2009) and can result in mental health problems (Lipsicas and Mäkinen, 2010; Torres, 2010).

People who adapt some pieces of the new culture while maintaining practices from their original culture are most successfully acculturated (Sue and Sue, 2012). Nonetheless, some of these variables may conflict, causing difficulties in the immigrant's life. For example, women who work tend to acculturate better than women who do not. Yet those women also have difficulties with their romantic relationships as a result (Grzywacz, Rao, Gentry, Marín, and Arcury, 2009).

Immigrants who are able to successfully acculturate while maintaining aspects from their culture of origin tend to be more successful in obtaining a college degree than those who only identify with the new culture or only maintain their old traditions without adapting to the new (Nekby, Rödin, and Özcan, 2009). Although it is often believed that people who learn a second language during or after puberty may have some biological constraints, new research has suggested other factors may also play important roles such as the level of acculturation (Jiang, Green, Henley, and Masten, 2009).

Latinos of low socioeconomic status tend to have more negative health conditions than other groups; yet when compared with non-Latino whites, they have a lower death rate (Abraído-Lanza, Chao, and Flórez, 2005). A confounding variable proposed to explain this phenomenon is the level of acculturation. Latinos with higher levels of acculturation are more likely to drink alcohol, smoke tobacco, and have an increased weight and body mass index (Abraído-Lanza *et al.*, 2005).

Related to health status in Latinos is the use of alternative medical procedures, such as home remedies and medical practices, folk medical syndromes, or culture-bound syndromes. Those who believe in culture-bound syndromes are often considered to be of low socioeconomic status (Mysyk, 1998). Because Western medicine is the most accepted healing method, anything else is viewed as inferior (Applewhite, 1995). Those who reside in areas where folk medical syndromes are common can identify them and are aware of what they entail, but not everybody acknowledges culture-bound syndromes because they want to avoid being considered illiterate and of low economic status (Mysyk, 1998).

In today's society, traditional healing methods within a culture are designed to treat certain conditions that often cannot be handled with one type of approach, such as pharmacology (Waldstein, 2008). The illnesses that form part of these systems are known as folk medical syndromes. These culture-bound syndromes are known by most people of a particular group and are treated by individuals who have natural and esoteric capability and knowledge (Trotter II, 1991). Although some of these syndromes and their symptoms are found across different cultures, their definition, interpretation, and treatment vary depending on the culture where the symptoms are experienced and identified (Landy, 1985).

The use of alternative therapies is not exclusive to a specific ethnicity or culture; however, the way they are accepted by different groups may vary substantially. Keegan (2000) conducted a study in which 60 Mexican Americans and 60 Anglo-Americans in the Rio Grande Valley of South Texas were asked about their use of alternative medical practices, their reaction toward these interventions, and whether they disclosed to their primary care physicians that they used these alternative methods. Both groups admitted to using alternative therapy methods; Mexican Americans used them twice as much as Anglo-Americans (Keegan, 2000). Mexican Americans were also more likely to disclose the use of these interventions to their primary care physician. These results show the presence of culture-bound syndromes in the Rio Grande Valley regardless of ethnicity (Keegan, 2000).

THEORY OF ACCULTURATION

A key concept in understanding cultures from cultural, cross-cultural, and indigenous perspectives is acculturation. Research on this topic has been fundamental in understanding multiculturalism and an individual's change of thoughts and behavior as this process occurs (Berry, 2003).

Initially, the concept of acculturation was defined from an anthropological perspective. Then scholars began to analyze it from a psychological approach.

Berry (2003) established a different way to perceive the process of acculturation. He proposed that instead of approaching it as a solely cultural or psychological phenomenon, it should include both, as culture affects human behavior but the process of acculturation varies by individual.

From a cultural approach, acculturation forms part of the process of change as one culture meets another; it causes changes in both the new and the established culture, and it may be influenced by the environment instead of cultural variables. It is a phenomenon that affects the established and the new culture. The acculturation process may occur at different times, depending on cultural factors, and the changes in the new culture may affect the established one. Professionals must be mindful in understanding culture before attempting to understand the individual (Berry, 2003).

Regarding acculturation from a psychological perspective, Berry (2003) noted that the individual is influenced by the new culture, which affects the original culture.

Since this change in the perception of acculturation, a new complex framework has been established. From a cultural perspective, it is necessary for professionals to understand concepts, principles, and characteristics of both cultural groups before contact occurred with each other. Then it is necessary to analyze the changes that resulted from the combination of both cultures. These changes may be small or have a great impact on the individual. Finally, research from this perspective needs to use qualitative ethnographic methodology (Berry, 2003).

In contrast, the individual approach should consider any psychological changes in both groups resulting from the integration of both cultures (Berry, 2003). Methods to evaluate acculturation from this perspective should be psychometric. Even though the changes may be mild and irrelevant to the person's general well-being, some are severe and may lead individuals to develop mental health problems.

Upon contact with the new culture, members of both groups know the reasons for their behaviors (e.g., a person migrates to a new culture looking for opportunity). However, they may still experience discomfort and unwanted unpleasant changes of behavior, leading to stress from the process

(Berry, 2003). Because of this, people look for different methods of dealing with acculturation.

Berry's theory offers four ways people cope with acculturation: assimilation, separation, integration, and marginalization (Berry, 1997). Assimilation is when the individual accepts the new culture and rejects the old culture. In separation, the individual does not accept the new culture and maintains the original. Integration refers to the individual who accepts the new culture and yet maintains the original. In marginalization, the individual rejects both the new and the original culture.

Immigrants have the option of coping with the acculturation process. Yet, their characteristics may cause the dominant group to discriminate against them, and they in turn may choose not to pursue integration and successful acculturation (Berry, 2001). This decision can affect the individual's cultural identity, which is considered an alternate approach to analyze the acculturation process (Berry, 2001). It is defined as the characteristics that identify people as members of a group, including beliefs, and that usually are overtly present when people are exposed to another culture rather than when they are living in the culture to which they belong (Berry, 2001).

Numerous studies have attempted to test Berry's model of acculturation (Schwartz and Zamboanga, 2008). In one, a sample of 436 students from a Miami university responded to a survey about their cultural identity and acculturation level (Schwartz and Zamboanga, 2008). The students were from Cuba, Colombia, Peru, Puerto Rico, and Nicaragua. The results showed some support for Berry's theory but some discrepancies became apparent, including two identified bicultural groups who differed in almost all of the variables, such as ethnic identity and cultural orientation (Schwartz and Zamboanga, 2008).

The acculturation process may also influence job performance of immigrants. Researchers conducted a study in Spain to explore the level of acculturation of immigrants from different countries and how this level influenced their work values (Osuna and Navarro, 2008). The sample consisted of 160 immigrants from Latin America, Eastern Europe, and Maghreb (Osuna and Navarro, 2008). They had diverse educations and averaged 34 years of age (Osuna and Navarro, 2008). Levels of acculturation and work values were measured using different tools (Osuna and Navarro, 2008). The researchers concluded that those with higher levels of acculturation had a stronger intrinsic motivation than those with lower levels (Osuna and Navarro, 2008). The highest intrinsic motivation was related to good relationships with peers and a job they found interesting (Osuna and Navarro, 2008). In terms of extrinsic motivation, the highest items had to do with salary and job stability (Osuna and Navarro, 2008). People in either separation or marginalization had low intrinsic motivation (Osuna and Navarro, 2008).

Immigrants who were identified as assimilated had medium intrinsic motivation, and those who were in the integrated group had high intrinsic motivation (Osuna and Navarro, 2008).

ACCULTURATION AND MENTAL HEALTH

Substantial research has been performed on mental health and multicultural issues which serves to create competency and allows for providers to understand the background and context of their patients (Draguns, 2008; Sue and Sue, 2012). However, this take on mental health focuses on addressing how the provider can help by using Western practices for sometimes non-Western needs (Sue and Sue, 2012). Furthermore, research demonstrates that the process of acculturation may cause mental health problems (Berdahl and Torres Stone, 2009; Davila, McFall, and Cheng, 2009; Lipsicas and Mäkinen, 2010; Smokowski and Bacallao, 2007; Torres, 2010). Those who successfully acculturate and yet maintain their traditional customs (i.e., become bicultural) tend to have fewer problems compared with those who acculturate and lose their original cultural practices (Sue and Sue, 2012). As Berry proposed (2003), people who integrate are those who have adopted the new culture while maintaining their own. These symptoms may exacerbate as a result of losing traditional medical practices that are not well accepted by Western medicine (Waldstein, 2008).

Torres (2010) studied methods for predicting depression in a Latino population by looking at their acculturation level, acculturative stress, and their coping mechanisms. The sample consisted of 148 Latinos, Latinas, and Hispanics who were asked to respond to a variety of items to measure the variables of the study (Torres, 2010). The results showed that the stress of acculturation was directly related to the understanding of the English language (Torres, 2010). Being competent in the English language was positively related to symptoms of depression (Torres, 2010). A positive correlation was established between acculturation stress and depression (Torres, 2010). Finally, people with higher depression levels considered themselves to have an Anglo orientation rather than a Latino one; those who considered themselves Latino had higher coping skills scores (Torres, 2010).

Another study by Berdahl and Torres Stone (2009) examined the use of mental health care facilities by Latinos, who are considered the least likely group to be insured (Berdahl and Torres Stone, 2009). The researchers showed some discrepancies in the use of these facilities: Mexicans used them the least, and Puerto Ricans used them the most (Berdahl and Torres Stone, 2009

The importance of being aware of cultural factors in an individual is crucial in treating mental health problems (Draguns, 2008; Sue and Sue, 2012).

Not being competent in multiculturalism or sensitive to these issues may result in misdiagnosis (Lizardi, Oquendo, and Graver, 2009; Trotter II and Chavira, 1997).

The practitioner also needs to be aware of alternative ways the person may deal with illness. Latinos' low use of mental health facilities (Berdahl and Torres Stone, 2009) may be because they are self-reliant (Berdahl and Torres Stone, 2009) and, instead, choose to use culture-bound treatments (Waldstein, 2008).

These folk medical practices can be influenced by acculturation and assimilation of the practitioners and the general community (Waldstein, 2008), but several regions in the United States exist, particularly those with a high number of immigrants, where these healing methods can still be identified and recognized as legitimate (Baer and Bustillo, 1993; Baer and Bustillo, 1998; Baer, Weller, De Alba Garcia, Glazer, Trotter, Patcher, and Klein, 2003; Trotter II and Chavira, 1997).

ACCULTURATION OF MEXICAN AMERICANS

Just as with the process of becoming and identifying as Mexican American, the acculturation and assimilation process is very complex and consists of usually several possible paths, influenced by numerous factors. As mentioned, some Mexican families resided in states that used to belong to Mexico and are now part of the United States. The transition of becoming part of a new country included a process of adapting to customs and cultural characteristics. However, because of the area, many practices remained the same. The English language was very important in adapting to the changes U.S. society required. The number of citizens who also spoke Spanish facilitated the acculturation process. For example, bilingual residents of California promoted learning English in addition to knowing Spanish (Train, 2013).

As is discussed in Chapter 6, the role of language is crucial to becoming acculturated to any society (Ottenheimer, 2013). However, social relationships facilitated through different generations, religious practices, and biology and health matters can also influence the acculturation process.

SOCIAL RELATIONSHIPS AND ACCULTURATION

The influence of family members, friends, and social relationships facilitates adaptation to any new culture. In fact, from an anthropological perspective, we know people first learn a culture into which they are born, and this learning occurs through information passed down from generations. Language, folk beliefs, values, and other characteristics are transmitted as part of the natural process of providing information the group considers to be important to subsistence. When a group is learning a new language, the same elements make the process easier and more effective. In other words, if family members are part of the culture, a person is more likely to successfully adapt than if that person did not have family members or close social relationships. In terms of Mexican Americans, however, this process can be affected by several factors, including discrepancies in acculturation level (Schofield, Parke, Kim, and Coltrane, 2008).

Some authors believe that people may develop mental health issues if the expectations their own culture sets for them differ from the expectations set by the mainstream culture. One example may be depression. As a result, minority groups such as Mexican Americans may be at a higher risk of experiencing life difficulties and even delinquent behaviors. The decision to drop out of school or attend college could be influenced by assimilation and acculturation (Knight, Vargas-Chanes, and Losoya, 2009).

ACCULTURATION AND EDUCATION

Mexicans have overall a lower level of education compared with their white Caucasian counterparts, which is a major risk factor in illness and mortality rates. People born in Mexico tend to live longer than those born in the United States. Research suggests, however, that they live longer with different types of impediments that hinder their daily activities (Garcia, Angel, Angel, Chiu, and Melvin, 2015).

Parental involvement plays a prominent role in academic achievement. One factor is parental expectation of children's performance at school. Children of parents with high expectations tend to obtain higher grades. Higher levels of acculturation are associated with a greater chance of academic success. Instead of solely attributing this success to adhering to U.S. culture and norms, length of time in and successful adaptation to the U.S. educational system may be responsible (Carranza, You, Chhuon, and Hudley, 2009).

The level of acculturation among Mexican Americans can be significant in regard to social behavior. In addition to playing a role in academic success and English language acquisition, acculturation can influence the way Mexican Americans respond to questions. Some response styles have been influenced by sociocultural factors, including level of acculturation, such as extreme response style (ERS), which is the tendency to respond at extreme levels on a response scale, and acquiescent response style (ARS), the tendency to generally agree. Mexican Americans who speak Spanish more frequently and have a greater knowledge of Spanish tend to utilize both extreme and acquiescent response styles. There may be other variables that influence the way Mexican Americans respond, such as levels of *familismo* or *machismo* (Davis, Resnicow, and Couper, 2011).

GENERATIONAL DIFFERENCES

Family members may go through the acculturation process in very different ways, so the level and type of acculturation may vary significantly. Whenever a difference in the level of acculturation existed between children and parents, there seemed to be conflict with fathers but not with mothers. This difference may be because mothers are move involved in childrearing while the role of fathers is more likely to be enforcing discipline. Conflicts between fathers and children also were exacerbated in cases where a well-established relationship did not exist to begin with (Schofield *et al.*, 2008).

Financial difficulties cause conflict among Mexican American couples, which can also lead to symptoms of depression. When symptoms of depression affect husbands, wives are shown to be particularly vulnerable, and the symptoms evoked negative emotions and perceptions about marriage (Helms, Supple, Su, Rodriguez, Cavanaugh, and Hengstebeck, 2014).

Acculturation is not defined as the mainstream culture substituting the original culture, but instead is now considered to be the integration of both cultures. Family loyalty is very important in the Mexican American population. In some studies, stronger relationships exist in Mexican American families than in Euro-American families (Leidy, Guerra, and Toro, 2010). Mutuality, to offer something to a person as a way to repay that person for what they have given, may be a better predictor of family loyalty than acculturation. This is particularly important when caring for elderly Mexican Americans (Kao and An, 2012).

Immigrant Mexican parents tend to have a similar level of identification toward the Mexican culture as the children. Children tend to identify with the American culture, however, significantly more than their parents. Conflict between parents and children of Mexican immigrant families is not attributed to cultural differences, but to developmental or generational factors (Nieri and Bermudez-Parsai, 2014). It appears that a higher acculturation level of parents was associated with adolescents' increased likelihood of marijuana use. However, discrepancies in level of acculturation between adolescents and their parents was not associated with increased marijuana use in adolescents. It seemed that parental monitoring was more significantly associated with marijuana use (Marsiglia, Nagoshi, Parsai, Booth, and González Castro, 2014).

BIOLOGY AND ACCULTURATION

As discussed, acculturation has an impact on Mexican Americans' health. In this section, the influence of acculturation and biology, health conditions, and general well-being is discussed.

Acculturation has been shown to be detrimental to the health of Mexican American immigrants. Diabetes is no exception. The Mexican American population has a higher risk of developing this condition, but the risk increases with the length of time in the United States. Body mass index (BMI) is the biological measure used to determine if a person is within normal weight, overweight, or clinically obese. BMI is often used to detect risk in developing several conditions, such as diabetes. People from other countries arrive in the United States with a lower BMI than those living here, but over time their BMI matches and supersedes the BMI of people already in the United States (Anderson, Zhao, Daniel, Hromi-Fiedler, Dong, Elhor Gbito, Wu, and Chow, 2016).

Fat mass of Mexican American women may be a stronger risk factor toward metabolic syndrome than physical activity. Metabolic syndrome refers to health problems related to metabolism, such as being overweight or obese and having high triglycerides, hypertension, and diabetes. Women more acculturated to the United States had higher BMI, higher levels of insulin while fasting, higher blood pressure, higher triglyceride levels, and more body fat than women less acculturated to U.S. society (Vella, Ontiveros, Zubia, and Bader, 2011). Recent research suggests acculturation may play a role in the frailty of older Mexican Americans. Frailty can entail general body weakness, decreased energy, psychomotor retardation, decreased physical activity, and weight loss. Although these symptoms could be a representation of mental health conditions, such as a depressive disorder, this syndrome does not necessarily involve feelings of sadness or depression or decreased interest or motivation.

Studies have revealed that a low level of acculturation to the United States protects health and well-being, while high levels have been detrimental to people's health in some cases. This correlation does not apply to the geriatric population, which seemed less vulnerable to frailty if it were more acculturated to U.S. society. Specifically, Mexican Americans aged 77 or older who spoke English and had more contact with Anglo-Americans were less likely to suffer from frailty. Unmarried older Mexican American males with less formal academic education and more chronic medical conditions were more susceptible to frailty. A confounding variable may be family size or contact with family members, as the Mexican American population is collectivistic (Masel, Howrey, and Peek, 2011). Older Mexican Americans with higher levels of acculturation also appeared less susceptible to developing metabolic syndrome (Gonzalez, Tarraf, and Haan, 2011).

Acculturation is also a factor in postpartum health care treatment and monitoring. Bicultural women, those acculturated to U.S. society while maintaining their cultural practices and views, were more likely to participate in postpartum treatment (Bermúdez-Parsai, Mullins Geiger, Marsiglia, and Coonrod, 2012).

Receiving preventive medical evaluations and treatment when required is not only dependent on level of acculturation. The availability of services and access to health insurance is a barrier that keeps many Mexican Americans from receiving these types of services (Salinas, de Heer, Lapeyrouse, Heyman, and Balcázar, 2015).

Gender differences can be seen in the relationship between level of acculturation and health. Mexican Americans with lower levels of acculturation appear to be healthier than those with higher levels, but this phenomenon applies to men more than women. As men become more acculturated, their health appears to deteriorate more than women's health (Gorman, Ghazal Read, and Krueger, 2010).

Low levels of physical activity have been associated with increased risk of developing cardiovascular conditions, diabetes, and other medical conditions. Mexican Americans living where the environment was conducive to physical activity were more likely to engage in it (Oluyomi, Whitehead, Burau, Symanski, Kohl, and Bondy, 2014).

ACCULTURATION MEASURES

The practical question is, how do we successfully and accurately measure level of acculturation of Mexican Americans? Without assuming and generalizing traits of people who have successfully acculturated to U.S. society, use of some basic measures of acculturation is important. We provide more information about these basic measures in Part II: Introduction to Clinical Topics. One of the most common is language. It is important, however, to consider other behaviors (Knight *et al.*, 2009).

Some scales can operationalize where people stand in terms of adapting to U.S. culture:

- The Multigroup Ethnic Identity Measure (Phinney, 1992). This measure requires respondents to answer 12 items on a Likert scale, ranging from 1 (strongly disagree) to 4 (strongly agree). It explores two dimensions of ethnic identity.
- The Acculturation Rating Scale for Mexican Americans-II (Cuellar, Arnold, and Maldonado, 1995), also known as the ARSMA-Version II, contains 30 items

divided into two major scales: American Orientation and Mexican Orientation. It also uses a Likert scale ranging from 1 (not at all) to 5 (extremely often or almost always).

- The Bicultural Involvement Questionnaire or BIQ (Szapocznik, Kurtines, and Fernandez, 1980) explores the level of acculturative and enculturative status using a scale from 1 (not comfortable behaviors) to 5 (very comfortable behaviors).
- The Short Acculturation Scale for Hispanics (Marín, Sabogal, VanOss Marín, Otero-Sabogal, and Pérez-Stable, 1987) identifies a person's preferred language used in different settings. The responses range from 1 (English only) to 5 (Spanish only).

SUMMARY

In this chapter, we discuss acculturation and its influence and effect on the Mexican American population. Research has provided information about the different obstacles and risks faced by Mexican Americans with different levels of acculturation. As clinicians, practitioners, academics, and researchers, it is important to consider these factors when working with this population to ensure the most effective approach. In Chapter 6, we look at the topic of language, which is somewhat related to acculturation. In the clinical topics section, we include more practical information pertaining to measurement and assessment levels of acculturation in a clinical setting.

Chapter 6

Language, Communication, and Mexican Americans

While working for an agency that provides assistance to people experiencing financial hardship, I spoke with a middle-aged woman having problems with her home's plumbing. She talked to me in Spanish, but mixed in some words in English, particularly those common in the United States which were most likely learned here, such as *tape* and *gas*. I used the word *tubo*, which in English means pipe. However, she did not understand what I was saying. I used the word in English, but she still didn't understand. I finally said she needed to change the *paipas*, which is a mix of English and Spanish, and she immediately recognized the word.

Combining languages as a way of expression is not unique to the areas surrounding the Mexico–United States border. It occurs during the adaptation and incorporation of two cultures into one and may be common in border towns (Ottenheimer, 2013). In this chapter, I examine language and the acculturation/assimilation process, first providing theoretical information about language and its relation to culture, something that can be achieved through the field of linguistic anthropology. Then I discuss language phenomena specifically within the Mexican American monolingual and bilingual communities, such as the process of combining English and Spanish to create a new form of communication.

LANGUAGE AND CULTURE

The study of linguistics has allowed scholars to understand language more deeply. We are now able to identify sounds that characterize each language and the way people develop the ability to produce such sounds. Great advances in the social sciences have allowed scholars to understand cultural characteristics of different groups. The field of anthropology can be defined as "the study of all people, at all times, and in all places" (Ottenheimer, 2013, p. 2). This field has been further divided into four major branches: physical anthropology, archaeology, cultural anthropology, and linguistic anthropology. The branch of physical or biological anthropology studies the origin of humans, human variations, and how humans have evolved. Archaeology studies ancient cultures. Cultural anthropology focuses on practices, beliefs, and a general examination of human behavior. Linguistic anthropology studies the use of language within a cultural and social setting (Ottenheimer, 2013).

If we already have the field of linguistics, why do we need linguistic anthropology? This field explores further the influence of language in society and culture and how society and culture affect language, something that is crucial to understand in the field of psychology.

LANGUAGE REFLECTING CULTURE

Through the study of linguistic anthropology, we can explore theories about how language works within a cultural context and how the culture shapes, changes, and determines language.

The concept of linguistic determinism suggests that language deeply affects people in the way they think about and perceive their surroundings. Many scholars have studied this topic, but two anthropologists are viewed as responsible for this theory. Edward Sapir was an anthropologist who studied under the instruction of Franz Boas, the father of American anthropology and the proponent of the concept of cultural relativism. Sapir was exposed to the idea of cultural relativism and extensively applied it to language. He proposed that even though it is possible to acquire general words and the classification of concepts through experience, once these words and basic components of language are embedded within a person, then that person is automatically disposed to perceive the world through the language he or she has learned to speak. Therefore, it is necessary to study and analyze language within its own context (Ottenheimer, 2013).

Benjamin Lee Whorf, an anthropologist who was Sapir's student, became very interested in studying the association between the way people perceive the world, the way they think, and the way they communicate and express their experiences. He proposed a concept known as the principle of linguistic relativity, which considered that people think in patterns influenced by the way a language's grammatical rules are set. It is extremely difficult, if not impossible, for a person to think in a way that is not consistent with a language's structure (Ottenheimer, 2013). The ideas of Sapir and Whorf were combined into what is now known as the Sapir–Whorf Hypothesis and states that language determines how a person thinks about and perceives the surrounding world (Myers, 2012).

Another concept is linguistic relativity, which suggests that languages are different and do not share similar elements. According to this model, every language has a randomness about it, and knowing one language does not guarantee the ability to foresee how another language will describe and structure the perceived world (Ottenheimer, 2013).

Noam Chomsky proposed that language is learned because humans are born with predetermined mental blocks that represent the functions of verbs, nouns, and other structures found in language (Myers, 2012).

LANGUAGE IS ALIVE

Language is often considered an immobile construct that has specific definitions, terms and rules which, if applied correctly, allow humans to successfully communicate with others. However, we know that language is constantly evolving, depending on social and cultural characteristics. These changes occur unconsciously and are simply adapted by the society or culture and added to the body of knowledge of any language.

Consider the following cases: Before extremely high buildings were constructed, there was no need to distinguish structures based on their height. The term *skyscraper* was developed to describe these buildings when they came into being. We can always create new words; however, in this case, the words *sky* and *scraper* were combined. Another example is the word *mouse*. The term was solely used to describe a small rodent; however, we now use it to describe a computer device. The word *spam* was used to describe a type of ham in a can. The term is now used to describe unwanted e-mail messages. Many similar examples exist in each language. Language evolves with culture and adapts to social changes.

NONVERBAL COMMUNICATION

When some people hear the word *language*, they think of verbal communication. Nonverbal gestures, however, can be as important as the words we choose. According to some scholars, over 60 percent of the communication of an idea is nonverbal (Ottenheimer, 2013). This percentage can also vary, depending on several factors. As discussed, some cultures value individualism more than collectivism, and vice versa. Research suggests that people from collectivist cultures tend to use a high-context form of communication, whereas people from individualistic cultures are more likely to use a low-context communication style (Merkin, 2015). Low-context communication consists of messages transmitted directly, while high-context is indirect and relies significantly on the context of the message, including nonverbal gestures. The Mexican American population generally values a collectivistic point of view, but the level of individualism or collectivism may be influenced by other factors, such as the level of acculturation. This observation is particularly important to keep in mind when offering clinical services, which we discuss in the second part of this book.

Consider the following example of the influence of nonverbal gestures on communication:

Laura, a 42-year-old Mexican American who speaks English and Spanish, goes to the local supermarket to purchase fruits and honey in order to prepare a fruit salad for her family. She asks a young man wearing a store uniform where the ingredients are, while standing about 10 feet from him. She speaks with a direct and strong voice and gets straight to the point. The young man points in the right direction and says, "Aisle 8," without looking at her face. The woman thanks him with the same tone she used in the question and moves away.

Depending on the context, the background, and other variables, anyone witnessing the scenario may have different opinions about this interaction. Some may think she went straight to the point to ensure she demonstrated she wanted to maintain her distance from the man. Others may think she was rude because she did not change her tone after receiving the information and because maintaining a distance of 10 feet may be too much, particularly because she is the one who needed assistance. Others may think the young man was very prudent and looked down and pointed so as not to make the woman feel uncomfortable. Maybe the young man reacted in such a way because the woman's assertiveness made him feel uncomfortable and he did not want to do anything that might have upset her.

Determining the factors at play in this interaction is complex usually consist of a combination of reasons. It is possible all of the circumstances above were occurring at the same time; it is also likely that cultural influences led each person to act in the way they did. The message may have been perceived differently if the nonverbal gestures and characteristics had been different. For example, imagine that the woman asked about the honey while smiling politely. Would the young man have reacted differently? What if the young man, despite her seriousness, would have looked at her and answered her using more words than just "Aisle 8"? Would the woman have been offended? Understanding that these reactions could have been greatly influenced by cultural factors, and considering that language and culture are imbedded, we can decrease the likelihood that we misunderstand interactions and communication styles.

TEX-MEX, SPANGLISH, AND CODE SWITCHING

It is important to remember the wide diversity found among people who consider themselves Mexican Americans. Not everybody speaks Spanish and not everyone mixes languages, but language mixing may occur depending on an individual's level of acculturation/assimilation and other social and cultural variables. The length of time someone has lived in the United States, the number of generations a person's family has been in the United States, and the level of education a person has had in the United States are among the variables that may influence language mixing (Otheguy and Stern, 2010).

Even within other ethnic groups, the English language can be very diverse. Monolingual English-speaking individuals may speak differently depending on where they reside. Consider two people from the same ethnic background, one originally from rural East Texas and the other originally from New York City. Some cultural and language differences are to be expected. When a person speaks another language, this diversity can be broader and can result in unique rules that apply only to the population represented (Otheguy and Stern, 2010). Particularly regarding language used by Mexican Americans, it is not uncommon to find individuals who speak only Spanish or only English, those who speak both languages but combine them to generate Spanglish, and those who only adapt certain words in English and combine those words with the Spanish language, such as in the case of the woman from the first scenario.

The terms *Tex-Mex* and *Spanglish* do not necessarily describe a person who is bilingual and is able to speak in both languages in different situations without mixing them. Usually, these terms describe the mixing of both languages into a third language within the same conversation and even within the same sentence (Otheguy and Stern, 2010). Tex-Mex is specific to the state of Texas. Spanglish is used to convey different notions. Some use it to refer to a Latino community language heritage; others prefer not to use it, as it may not include all of the linguistic elements that a single term can entail. Thus, some scholars prefer to use the terms *Chicana* or *Chicano Spanish* or *Chicana* or *Chicano English* (Sánchez-Muñoz, 2013).

Code switching in some ways is Spanglish (Dumitrescu, 2014). This concept describes incorporating words from two languages within the same sentences (Otheguy and Stern, 2010). This type of communication may be considered colloquial and disorganized, but several rules are imbedded in this system and does not necessarily substitute any word from a sentence for its corresponding word of the opposite language. Someone code switching may say "*me duele la head*," which translates to "my head hurts." Notice the only word in English is "head." This sentence follows the grammatical rules of Spanish and would be a grammatically correct sentence in Spanish if the word *head* were in Spanish. Furthermore, if any of the other words were changed to English, the sentence would not necessarily be Spanglish. If a person said "*Mi cabeza* hurts," which also means "my head hurts," this sentence would not follow the normal flow of Spanglish. Thus, code switching makes Spanglish a complex system and in some ways, an independent language that follows its own rules.

Spanglish has become more popular and recognized by linguists and other scholars, and it has become a language used by some contemporary literary authors (Dumitrescu, 2014). Nevertheless, some people think labeling it as Spanglish can single out people who use it as not speaking "correct" or "acceptable" Spanish (Otheguy and Stern, 2010). Most linguists and scholars view Spanglish as important in understanding human communication when using a blend of languages and cultures (Dumitrescu, 2014). Some people may still consider Spanglish inappropriate, however (Otheguy and Stern, 2010). The use of books in the classroom written in Spanglish can help educate students to not only understand the way languages can be combined, but also to describe cultural characteristics (Postma, 2013).

Because Spanish is spoken in a variety of countries, its use in the United States can generate different methods of communication. For example, a Spanish-speaking individual from Mexico who resides in the United States is likely to use a different form of Spanish than an immigrant from Spain. Because of these differences, there are different varieties of popular Spanish. The way Spanish is used will depend on the region. For example, even though there is a general term to identify the noun *bus*, which is *autobus*, the vehicle has many other names, depending in the location, such as *microbus, guagua, and camión* (Otheguy and Stern, 2010).

In the United States, individuals also use some words in English without using them in an English context. People may learn how to say certain words based on the way they hear them and identify them as nouns. These words may be viewed as a form of code switching, but the person learned how to say some words in English based on how they sounded. An example of this is *jáiscul* instead of high school (Otheguy and Stern, 2010).

Code switching and other language phenomena primarily develop within a social context and are not acquired consciously. Even when adults attempt to inculcate their children to speak two independent languages, children use other language strategies to communicate with their peers (Kyratzis, Tang, and Koymen, 2009). Socially speaking, this practice has not always been viewed positively, particularly in settings where authority figures, such as teachers in academic settings, do not speak Spanish or understand the language dynamics of code switching. Thus, in several instances, individuals who utilized these types of communication forms were viewed negatively or viewed as inferior (Kyratzis *et al.*, 2009). A commonly held belief has been that bilingual education was detrimental to learning the English language; however, more scholars have determined that a structured bilingual education promotes the learning of both languages in conjunction (Palmer, Mateus, Martínez, and Henderson, 2014). A main obstacle to promoting this type of education is the continuing perception about Spanish and bilingualism. Some teachers may not even be aware of their own biases toward students who are bilingual and use code switching. Yet, they may not offer instruction promoting these characteristics because they are influenced by preferential monolingual instruction. In addition to teachers' cultural and language limitations, children could possibly be led to become more insecure about their way of communicating and could feel a cultural acceptance conflict (Ek, Sánchez, and Quijada Cerecer, 2013).

THE SPANISH LANGUAGE IN A MEXICAN AMERICAN CULTURAL CONTEXT

Spanish and Immigrants

Language and its value can take many forms depending on the setting and the circumstances in which it is evaluated. People who do not speak English value those who speak it with a limited vocabulary and a sharp accent. Those who speak in this fashion may value those who speak with an English accent. In the same way, the Spanish language can be perceived differently depending on the context. In the Rio Grande Valley where I reside, I have witnessed a couple of interesting phenomena. Fewer children seem to speak Spanish, and for a variety of reasons they seem to not value this language such as peer pressure, the desire to speak in the language of the TV shows they watch, and the sometimes erroneous perception that only by devaluing Spanish will they be able to learn the English language and attain a degree from an institution of higher education. The second phenomenon is that many people consider themselves bilingual without dominating the Spanish language. The question I often get is, should those people really consider themselves bilingual? Should they learn how to speak an impeccable Spanish to be considered as such? Depending on the need and the purpose of the language, the answer varies. If a person is going to be a translator at a hospital, then they may be better off having an extensive knowledge of the languages to be translated. However, if the purpose is to help people find the right item at a supermarket, the demands of dominating a language may not be as high.

Spanish is one of the most widely spoken languages in the world. Because the U.S. population has been predominantly formed by immigrants, it is not surprising that Spanish is commonly spoken in the United States. In fact, some people consider Spanish the "second national language" (Silva Gruesz, 2012). Unfortunately, the use of this language has been affected by anti-immigrant attitudes influenced in part by political forces (Ek et al., 2013). This type of discourse produces negative consequences for those who migrate from other countries to the United States and may lead them to reject characteristics that they may associate with the status of immigrant, including language (Ek et al., 2013).

Speaking Spanish has been associated with low socioeconomic status and ignorance. Some may view this as an inability to learn the official language of the United States, which can inaccurately be considered as a resistance to becoming part of the new country. In contrast, Spanish-speaking people viewed this attitude as a way of being oppressed and considered speaking Spanish as a way of protesting and expressing their pride in belonging to an ethnic and cultural group. As mentioned, Américo Paredes, an eminence in Mexican American cultural studies and folklore, expressed to me in an interview that people refused to learn English because they thought they would be viewed as cultural traitors. Américo Paredes and others think the best way to change the perception of the Spanish language is to first learn English, then emerge in the U.S. culture and propose change from within the system. Although some areas promote bilingualism and biculturalism, several regions still do not consider them valuable to U.S. society.

In addition to a negative perception of the Spanish language, some Spanish-speaking people also criticize the use of anything that is not considered "standard" or "correct" Spanish. This communication includes proper grammar, syntax, and pronunciation rules. Every way that deviates from this correctness is considered to be wrong and is associated with ignorance, as this correct form of Spanish is taught in academic settings. Consider the use of superlative adjectives in the English language. We use the word *good* to describe something that is acceptable, preferred, or positive. We can say, "Speaking many languages in a multicultural world is *good*." If we wanted to compare this with another characteristic, we can say, "Speaking many languages in a multicultural world is *better than* speaking only one language." Lastly, we can say, "Speaking many languages in a multicultural world is *the best* thing anyone can do." Under some circumstances, some people may break these grammatical rules and use *more better* rather than *better* or *best.* "Speaking many languages in a multicultural world is *more better* than speaking one language." This phrase is not correct and does not follow the traditional structure of the English language. Nevertheless, some people use it to successfully express what they want to share with others, which is the ultimate goal of communication.

It is important to understand the general perception about the varieties of Spanish in the United States, including Spanglish or code switching. Individuals who speak only Spanish may be viewed negatively. People may wonder why others do not speak English, may assume things about those people's lives, and may associate this behavior with negative factors (e.g., they are not intellectually competent to learn English; they are refusing to learn how to communicate in English as a form of protest against U.S. society; they want to promote solely Spanish so that they can reduce the use of English and substitute English with Spanish). Those who use standard Spanish, whether they are able to communicate in English or not, usually view any other version of Spanish as illegitimate, causing division. Just as in the example presented at the beginning of this chapter, it is sometimes important to mix English with Spanish in order to communicate, but this mixing is not always well perceived (Rangel, Loureiro-Rodríguez, and Moyna, 2015).

Keep in mind that language is a reflection of culture, and different layers of analysis exist when comparing and appreciating the languages. Ultimately, people express themselves to share information and communicate ideas and needs at different levels. Even if a person does not speak standard Spanish, he or she may still get a point across to another person.

Because of the sometimes oppressiveness of using a language, some may feel subdued if they do not speak English, which could add to factors that make Spanish-speaking Mexican Americans feel underprivileged. Mexican Americans able to learn English may have better opportunities, but they may still have to overcome obstacles to feeling fully accepted by society.

Learning a new language does not mean losing the ability to communicate in the native language, or that the person's cultural practices have to completely change. Instead of promoting bilingualism and biculturalism, speaking Spanish sometimes is viewed as one more obstacle to learning English.

In order to guide people to learn English while they maintain Spanish, several factors need to come together. One of the main obstacles to learning English is that not enough competent people are able to teach immigrants proper English. Some of those responsible for teaching English to Mexican American immigrants have their own biases about this population. Terms like *Tarzan English* have been used to describe how some immigrant children communicate with English-speaking people. This form of communication consists of talking in a broken manner while mixing English and Spanish (e.g., phrases like, "Me no speak English."). Because of the term *Tarzan*, this form of expression is associated with ignorance rather than a person's efforts to express ideas and communicate with others (Gallo, Link, Allard, Wortham, and Mortimer, 2014). People who use this kind of label are not prepared or trained to teach this population. However, those specialized in teaching English as a Second Language (ESL) tend to be more culturally sensitive and attempt to view this process as an opportunity to assist people in developing and in acquiring the English language, thus appreciating and respecting immigrants' efforts.

SUMMARY

In this chapter, we discuss concepts related to the language of Mexican Americans. The methods in which Mexican Americans communicate vary depending on different factors, including level of acculturation, length of time spent in the United States, family history, and the location where a person resides. Appreciating the different forms of communication used by this population is crucial to becoming culturally sensitive and competent in working with Mexican Americans.

In the next chapters, we speak more in depth about how to incorporate this information in a practical manner and within a clinical setting. This ends the first section of the book, which presented theoretical and historical information about Mexican Americans. In the second section, we present clinical topics.

Part II

Introduction to Clinical Topics

As a clinician, I became very interested in offering culturally competent psychological services to the Mexican American population. Having received training in multicultural counseling and psychological practices, I believed I had been prepared for this job. After I graduated, I realized there is still a lot to do and learn in order to be able to offer competent services to this population. In the following chapters, you will read about clinical topics pertaining to the Mexican American population. Some of the information is general, and we will cover several clinical topics that apply to different populations. The objective is to create awareness regarding the need for culturally sensitive services when working with Mexican Americans.

Chapter 7

Mexican Americans and Mental Health

A few years ago, I taught Abnormal Psychology at the undergraduate level, covering different types of mental disorders in a general way. I always warned the students not to try to diagnose themselves or anyone else with the information covered in class. However, I heard many students talking about people they knew who suffered certain symptoms. I found these comments interesting because in clinical settings people have a difficult time accepting that others, including those we love, may suffer from a mental illness.

Among other things, I sometimes offer clinical consultations when people have questions about mental health treatment. Even though they are usually receptive to the idea of talking to someone about their problems (receiving individual counseling or psychotherapy), their attitude changes when they hear they may suffer from a mental disorder. Even after explaining that the symptoms they are complaining about appear consistent with any given psychopathology, people often seem resistant to accepting a diagnosis. On one occasion, after assessing and explaining to a person that he had symptoms characteristic of bipolar disorder, he stated that he did not believe so and preferred to hear that he suffers from diabetes rather than from a mental illness.

Psychopathology is based on constructs and some self-reported, subjective symptoms, such as feeling depressed for most of the day, more days than not (American Psychiatric Association, 2013), and mental health treatments oftentimes do not seem to be immediately relieving, leading to suspicions about the diagnosis. In this example, the person would consider treatment for this pathology only if it was very affordable or free, which made me change my perception about how the general population views mental health.

Shortly after that, I decided to offer free psychological services at a local clinic. People complied with treatment and showed interest in these services. Unfortunately, the program was not able to continue, and the clinic began to require clients to pay a small fee for the same services. At that time, a clear decline in attendance and participation took place. The question I asked myself and I encourage you to think about is, why? Is it possible people simply did not want to pay for services they did not consider to be essential? Would they have reacted the same way if a physician asked them to return for services? What about the fact that the services were at first free, and then had a cost? If this had not occurred and we had charged the clients a fee at the beginning, would they have complied continuously?

In this chapter, I provide information about strategies that can help Mexican American clients be more engaged in their mental health treatment. However, it is important to first identify some of the obstacles that arise when offering mental health treatment and the general perception Mexican Americans have about mental health.

The Mexican American population, just like other groups in the United States, does not view mental health treatments the same way as health care services (Office of the Surgeon General; Center for Mental Health Services; National Institute of Mental Health, 2001). They may correctly feel these services are necessary to avoid getting sick, but those who have recognized and identified mental health symptoms that can affect their general functioning and can even experience a high risk of danger may still not be as receptive to treatment.

MENTAL HEALTH AND LATINOS

The mental health system in the United States has been developing over the past few decades. In the realm of multicultural services and cultural sensitivity, important efforts have been made to include cultural factors in mental health treatment. One of the objectives is to engage members from these groups to participate in evidence-based mental health treatment, such as counseling or psychotherapy from a licensed practitioner. However, some ethnic and cultural groups may view mental health treatments as no more effective than non-Western alternative methods of treatment, such as a *curandero*, or just talking to an older person from the family. Without discrediting other forms of emotional assistance, it is important to mention the research and evidence that supports the current interventions used in contemporary mental health.

MENTAL HEALTH OF MEXICAN AMERICANS

In the United States, it is not uncommon for Mexican Americans to lack knowledge regarding mental health services (Office of the Surgeon General; Center for Mental Health Services; National Institute of Mental Health, 2001). Some of this lack of information comes from the negative perception of mental illness in the Mexican American community as a result of proscriptions and rules set by social groups and cultural customs. It is crucial, therefore, for mental health professionals to understand and apply multicultural strategies when providing counseling and psychotherapy to a minority Mexican or to a person of Mexican origin who resides in the United States, which has large diversities within the same ethnic classification.

SOME FACTS ABOUT MEXICAN AMERICAN MENTAL HEALTH

Because the Mexican American population has several social disadvantages, it has a higher risk than other populations of experiencing mental health issues and of encountering problems accessing treatment. Factors include lack of health care resources, low socioeconomic status, limitations with the English language, prejudice and discrimination, and low levels of education, including higher dropout rates (Valencia-García, Simoni, Alegría, and Takeuchi, 2012). Mexican American women also are more at risk of negative mental health treatment outcomes (Valencia-García *et al.*, 2012). Being able to successfully integrate into U.S. society may increase the chances of receiving mental health treatment, reducing the risk and permanence of suffering from symptoms of anxiety and depression (Valencia-García *et al.*, 2012).

Within the Mexican American population, those who were concerned about being discriminated against, had a decrease in income, and faced difficulties accessing mental health treatment were more likely to report symptoms of depression (Leung, LaChapelle, Scinta, and Olvera, 2014).

Furthermore, Mexican Americans suffering from symptoms of depression are more likely to seek help from a physician, an indigenous healer, or a family member than to explore specific mental health treatment from a mental health professional (Leung *et al.*, 2014).

Mexican American adults' emotional problems may have their roots in childhood and adolescence. Compared with other ethnic, social, and cultural groups, Mexican American adolescents are considered to be more at risk of experiencing difficulties with academic performance, in developing intense problems with mood and emotions, and in displaying conduct problems (Gonzales, Dumka, Millsap, Gottschall, McClain, Wong, *et al.*, 2012). Mexican American adolescents may be at risk of symptoms of depression due to several factors, including bicultural stress or difficulties adapting to a new mainstream culture while coping with the demands of the culture of origin (Piña-Watson, Llamas, and Stevens, 2015). Problems that can arise include prejudice and discrimination, language difficulties, and financial hardship (Piña-Watson *et al.*, 2015). Mexican Americans are also at a higher risk than other ethnic groups of consuming illicit substances (Gonzales *et al.*, 2012). If this risk is added to other potential factors, such as residing near the border with Mexico where drugs may be more easily accessible and affordable, the risks increase significantly.

Another important factor to consider when addressing mental health in Mexican Americans is the possibility of working away from home or migrating to work away from the person's family. Particularly with undocumented Mexican immigrants, mental health issues may arise as a result of the constant exposure to anxiety and stress caused by their legal status (Sullivan and Rehm, 2005). Research also suggests that whenever Mexican men migrate by themselves and leave their families behind, the women experience more stress, leading to an increased risk of mental health issues. Their situation forces them to take on a more masculine role that is not consistent with their cultural formation and practices. They may feel distress and general mental health problems if they have to take on roles for which their culture or social rules have not necessarily prepared them (Wilkerson, Yamawaki, and Downs, 2009).

CLASSIFICATION OF MENTAL HEALTH

It is not uncommon for individuals to have different ideas and priorities about the concept of mental health. Some may think of psychopathology and accurate diagnostic procedures, and others may consider primary, secondary, or tertiary interventions in order to understand the concept. For the purpose of this chapter and before including further information about this topic, it is important to subdivide this section into the following three areas:

1. Psychopathology and diagnosis, including some of the most common mental disorders within the Mexican American population, such as depressive disorders and anxiety disorders.
2. Treatment and interventions, such as individual and group psychotherapy and counseling, psychotherapeutic education and prevention, and assessments and evaluations.
3. Resources, an understanding of obstacles, and strategies to help engage Mexican American clients to receive mental health services.

Psychopathology

Mental disorders or psychopathology is often misunderstood, misguided, and misused. People who experience sadness may erroneously utilize the term *depression* to describe their state of mind. However, an actual mental health condition must include symptoms that are impairing, distressing, and dysfunctional. Some of the most common conditions in the Mexican American population include depressive disorders and anxiety disorders. However, some mental illnesses are also present that may occur at similar rates in other populations or groups, such as schizophrenia, which is believed to be suffered by about 1 percent of the population (American Psychiatric Association, 2013).

Schizophrenia is one of the most severe mental health conditions. It is usually characterized by hallucinations and is mainly treated with drug therapy. The symptoms can be reduced with psychotropic medication, such as clozapine, and the combination of drug therapy with other types of therapy can help people carry on normal lives (Durão and De Mello e Souza, 2006).

Mental illnesses induced or caused by substance use can also occur in this population (American Psychiatric Association, 2013). Substance-use disorder consists of several types of behaviors that indicate the person is being affected by these substances yet continues to use them. The person may also develop a substance-induced condition or a mental illness triggered by the substance use. In some cases, a person's symptoms may go away and he or she may return to normal as soon as the substance use stops. Regardless of the discontinuation of the substance, however, some individuals continue to experience symptoms, and these symptoms become chronic (American Psychiatric Association, 2013).

There are several factors that can influence development of these mental illnesses. Any type of traumatic event can result in a psychological disorder. This disorder can be reflected in dissociation as a result of a defense mechanism and a coping skill to deal with the symptoms caused by the trauma (Martinez-Taboas and Bernal, 2000).

Another factor that can influence the development of a mental illness in any type of individual, regardless of ethnicity, is the circumstance experienced by those of low socioeconomic status. Such circumstances can lead a person to have more stress, anxiety, and other symptoms. One of the major characteristics that can trigger a psychological disorder is unemployment (Ortega, Canino, and Alegria, 2008). As a result of unemployment and other social problems related to a lack of assistance and resources, individuals can also fall into the use of illicit substances, thus abusing them and eventually altering their nervous system and their brain's physiological processes, thereby, in some cases, even developing psychosis. Substance abuse can increase the probability of developing psychological symptoms (Ortega *et al.*, 2008). Finally, some lifestyles can trigger a psychological disorder's symptoms as a result of stressors and the increased probability of experiencing difficult social situations.

Attitude of Mexican Americans toward Psychopathology

Like other populations, Mexican Americans historically do not openly accept psychopathology or mental illness as something that is part of today's society. Those who receive mental health treatment (whether psychotherapy, counseling, or psychiatric interventions) are often viewed as unable to address their problems without assistance due to a lack of skill or capacity (Office of the Surgeon General; Center for Mental Health Services; National Institute of Mental Health, 2001). As in the example at the beginning of this chapter, people treated for medical conditions are not viewed as negatively as those who suffer from mental illness. In addition to a stigma about the diagnosis and psychopathology, negative impressions exist about mental health interventions. As mentioned, Mexican Americans suffering from mental, emotional, or behavioral problems are more likely to seek help from a primary care physician, a neighbor or someone they trust, or a folk healer rather than getting treatment from someone who specializes in addressing these conditions (Leung *et al.*, 2014). This attitude may be the result of several factors. Those individuals may not feel as negatively perceived because of their psychological or psychiatric impairment if they do not formally receive treatment from a specialist and instead just receive treatment from a primary care physician. Also, they may feel reluctant to specifically share very intimate and personal information to a stranger and may feel more comfortable talking to someone close to them. Because of misconceptions about mental health treatment, it is possible that people may not believe the treatment to be legitimate or useful.

Hopelessness

General research on depression has identified several symptoms that may accompany the diagnosis and that allow for the diagnosis to be easily identified. One of the most important symptoms is hopelessness, particularly because it has been directly associated with increased risk of suicide (Durant, Mercy, Kresnow, Simon, Potter, and Haniniond, 2006). When working with the Mexican American population, it is important to assess for different symptoms of depression, as the difficulties that members of this group experience increase the probability that these symptoms will emerge.

Mexican American women tend to experience more mental health issues than their male counterparts. Yet, they usually have more difficulty accessing mental health services (Marsiglia, Kulis, Garcia Perez, and Bermudez-Parsai, 2011). One of the reasons women seem more affected is that not working and having large households appears to be significant in the development of hopelessness, something that is not uncommon in some Mexican American people (Marsiglia *et al.*, 2011). Traditional Mexican American women may take care of their household, may dedicate most of their time to raising their children, and may not be able to work due to these responsibilities, which increases the risk of developing this symptom. Additionally, individuals who lack a strong support system may be more at risk of hopelessness, particularly those who are not acculturated into U.S. society, do not speak English, and have recently arrived into this country (Marsiglia *et al.*, 2011). Resiliency based on cultural identity and optimism appeared to be protective factors against hopelessness in the Mexican American population (Marsiglia *et al.*, 2011).

The mental health system in the United States consists of several components that, if orderly, can complement each other. For example, to treat some types of psychosis, it is important for the individual being affected to be seen by a psychiatrist. However, the individual might require some psychotherapy to learn skills for coping with the psychotic symptoms.

With advances in psychopharmacology, better ways to treat mental illnesses exist, with fewer side effects. However, psychotherapeutic treatment in a multicultural fashion obtains better results, even if the mental illness is treated with psychopharmacology (Durão and De Mello e Souza, 2006).

An important part of multicultural counseling is the understanding and use of cultural sources of support the individual possesses and avoiding seeing this strategy as useless or inferior (Ulin, 2007). For example, folk medicine might be used to treat certain illnesses, including psychological ones. It may not be the best method, and the therapist may even consider it harmful, but understanding such practices can be a great benefit when applying the therapist's own strategy and psychological treatment (Baer, Weller, De Alba Garcia, Glazer, Trotter, Pachter, and Klein, 2003).

The Importance of Multicultural Counseling in Mexican Americans

The field of psychology and its clinical application is complex and robust. Several areas specialize in a variety of human behavioral aspects. Even though counseling and clinical approaches to pathologies and behavioral problems have existed since the beginning of the century, some changes have also occurred in accordance with technological advances and discoveries in related areas such as medicine, neurology, physiology, and the social sciences, such as anthropology and sociology.

MULTICULTURAL COUNSELING

A need exists to shape the field of multicultural counseling based on characteristics that surround the population and the location where this science is being applied. Cultural customs and other societal components form an essential part of each individual in a specific group. In countries like the United States, other sociocultural effects arise as a result of migration and the variety of cultural and ethnic groups that establish themselves in a common location. Because the United States is a multicultural country, it has been forced to implement a different strategy in order to understand issues when one considers the backgrounds of individuals and aspects of their cultural origin. To resolve problems related to the misconception of cultural practices and cultural influence in an individual, multicultural counseling strategies have been developed and adjusted to today's theories of psychotherapy and mental health in general (Comas-Diaz, 2006; Worthington, Soth-McNett, and Moreno, 2007).

SOCIAL OBSTACLES FOR IMMIGRANTS

Language barriers and communication problems are major obstacles for immigrants of Mexican descent in understanding and adapting to a new culture. Other major social problems and individual characteristics, however, also affect the lifestyle of Mexicans and Mexican Americans residing in the United States (Torres, 2004).

The motivation behind an individual's migration to the United States is essential in understanding the perception of the individual toward the country of origin and the new country (Comas-Diaz, 1998). Most commonly people go to the United States to find employment, but this does not mean they are ready to leave their country of origin's lifestyle, practices, or customs and immediately adapt to a new lifestyle (Garcia and Saewyc, 2007).

Latinos face stereotypes established even before they arrive in the United States. Stereotypes affect the individual directly by describing him or her negatively, and stereotyping individuals without completely understanding the person's social context can be extremely harmful. For example, it's important to know if someone from Mexico is from a rural area or a metropolis or to know which country a Latin-American immigrant is from. Without this information, an individual will not experience the individualistic feeling that is otherwise portrayed in the different institutions of the United States (Worthington et al., 2007).

KEY INTERVENTIONS

Considering that several mental health issues of Mexican Americans arise during middle childhood and adolescence, interventions during those years can decrease the impact of these issues and may even resolve them early enough to prevent significant impairment. The following are some examples of the models used to address Mexican American behavioral and emotional concerns, considering several factors. These are not the only models to use when working with Mexican Americans, but should be considered for a multifaceted and multicomponent approach that includes sociocultural variables.

The Bridges–Puentes intervention is a strategy to help integrate the child's or adolescent's experiences at home and at school (also with the involvement of the parents) to successfully transition through middle school to high school (Gonzales et al., 2012). Instead of considering a person's growth and development from a single perspective (and the person's problems that arise through the process), consider them as a result of a mixture of forces, influences, and settings. In the case of Mexican Americans, these factors may refer to their migratory status, socioeconomic status, and acculturation levels (Gonzales et al., 2012).

Another model that can serve as an intervention to address symptoms of depression is the Mexican American Problem Solving (MAPS) program. It targets Mexican American children in fourth and fifth grade, focusing on developing abilities to resolve problems, and it is delivered after school. A component also involves assisting mothers in their homes (Gonzales et al., 2012).

There are three main elements in this model. Adaptation Risk considers any factors that serve as context, including demographic information, level of acculturation, general functioning of the family, and the location and type of residence where the family lives. It considers experiences from the past that could have influenced the child's mental health, the child's characteristics, such as self-esteem, and his or her ideas about health. The second element, Intervention, pertains to general information about health (including problem-solving focus information), emotional encouragement and backing, and control for making right decisions. All the problem-solving information is focused on the issues or problems the child or family may be experiencing. The third element, Outcomes, is the result of the implementation of the intervention. It can include a general measure of symptomatology of depression, academic performance, family communication and interaction, and other problems that may have appeared as a result of depression (Gonzales et al., 2012).

Research has shown that several protective factors can assist in risk reduction of Mexican American adolescents suffering symptoms of depression. One, as generally indicated in the previous models, is family support, specifically the closeness and well-established connection with the adolescent's female caregiver (Piña-Watson *et al.*, 2015).

Social support can be as important for elder Mexican Americans. However, additional factors can influence the presence of symptoms of depression. Older Mexican American males appear to be more at risk of developing depression if they reside in neighborhoods with a low proportion of Mexican American residents. In contrast, where there is a high rate of Mexican American neighbors, there is a lower risk of these symptoms. This correlation does not appear to affect older Mexican American women in the same way. Although there appears to be a similar correlation between the number of Mexican American neighbors and the presence of symptoms of depression, the effects do not appear to be significant (Gerst, Miranda, Eschbach, Sheffield, Peek, and Markides, 2011). One explanation is the value of cultural contexts and practices in older Mexican Americans, something that has to be taken into consideration when working with this population. Another important factor to consider when assessing symptoms of depression in older Mexican Americans is the level of acculturation. As mentioned, acculturation has a negative correlation with mental health; the more acculturated a person is, the more mental health problems he or she is likely to experience (Abraído-Lanza *et al.*, 2005). This relationship, however, does not appear to be consistent throughout different ages. Older adults (75 years or older) appear to not follow this pattern and instead seem to be more vulnerable to experiencing mental health issues if they are less acculturated. Older Mexican American immigrants appear to be more at risk of experiencing symptoms of depression compared with older U.S. natives (Gerst, Al-Ghatrif, Beard, Samper-Ternent, and Markides, 2010). Older Mexican Americans experience difficulties accessing treatment to address depression. For example, when compared to older white Caucasian Americans, older Mexican Americans experience some discontinuation and a gap in mental health services through their primary care, including appropriate diagnosis and treatment (Hinton, Apesoa-Varano, González, Aguilar-Gaxiola, Dwight-Johnson, Barker, *et al.*, 2012).

In addition, different minority groups at the college level (including Mexican Americans) may be at a higher risk of experiencing symptoms of depression when they attend a college in which they are not the majority. However, in settings in which they are the majority group within a college or university, they continue to report higher instances of symptoms of depression, such as loneliness and hopelessness, than their white counterparts attending a white majority college or university (Smith, Chesin, and Jeglic, 2014).

POTENTIAL OBSTACLES

One of the major problems Latinos encounter in the treatment of mental disorders is a lack of resources and information. Although some folk medical syndromes can affect an individual's perception of reality, and that eventually can induce psychological symptoms such as *nervios* or *susto*, individuals could mistake these syndromes with an actual psychological/ psychiatric diagnosis (Baer *et al.*, 2003).

It is important to educate the population about mental disorders and psychological/psychiatric treatment that can reduce symptoms. One of the most common limitations among individuals from Hispanic/Latino communities is the proscription and stigma about mental disorders and psychiatric patients. These attitudes are usually caused by a lack of information and a reluctance to admit these types of problems exist within every U.S. community. This information should explain the difference between suffering from a pathological condition and experiencing symptoms of that pathology. Symptoms characterize different psychological disorders, but every person in the community has experienced such symptoms.

In addition, to show the population the characteristics of mental disorders and possible treatments, it is important to provide services related to pathologies. People might need to receive some sort of psychotherapy or counseling about an issue they are experiencing. Going through a session with a mental health professional can remove stereotyping and proscription about this topic.

When working with Mexican American adolescents experiencing bicultural stress resulting in a general dissatisfaction and symptoms of depression, involving the adolescents' caregivers in the treatment has been shown to be effective (Piña-Watson, Llamas, and Stevens, 2015). The adolescents may regain life satisfaction and experience a reduction of symptoms, possibly triggered by the strong impact of family support, particularly from the female caregiver or mother (Piña-Watson *et al.*, 2015).

The Mexican American population has to overcome several limitations in order to receive competent and appropriate mental health treatment, including a lack of bilingual (English/Spanish) mental health professionals throughout the country. Even if a clinician speaks Spanish in daily life, this communication may not directly transfer to a clinical setting. And even if the clinician speaks Spanish, the client may use a different "type" of Spanish, resulting in an ineffective intervention. A way to address this problem would be to become culturally sensitive to the needs of the clients. In addition to needing bilingual clinicians, there is also a need for culturally competent professionals who can work with the Mexican American population (Torres, Parra-Medina, and Johnson, 2008). Understanding the cultural background and context of Mexican American clients can make a difference between being unable to establish an appropriate rapport and engaging clients to receive mental health treatment when they need it.

SUMMARY

In this chapter, we discuss the mental health of Mexican Americans. We present some of the most common psychopathologies or mental conditions that some members of this population may experience, some methods to address these conditions, and potential obstacles and barriers that keep Mexican Americans from engaging in, participating in, and receiving appropriate treatment. In the following chapters, we talk in more detail about the different approaches to demonstrating cultural sensitivity and the ability to show cultural competency when working with this population. In Chapter 8, we explore the clinical interview, how to approach it, and how to avoid areas that may be counterproductive.

Chapter 8

The Clinical Interview

I was told an advanced student I supervised, who offered psychological services, had struggled to conduct a clinical interview with a Mental Status Exam, which we define here later. His client was a 45-year-old Spanish-speaking married female who identified herself as Mexican American. He said she was very guarded and did not want to speak much about her problem. The student felt inexperienced, and his attempts to engage the client failed. He then began to feel nervous, which she detected, telling him it was better if she saw someone with more experience. We reviewed the interview process and the questions asked, and the intern mentioned that all of the client's responses focused on her family. When he asked how the situation made her feel, for example, she kept saying the situation was distressing to her three daughters.

The student said he was also concerned about the client's Mental Status Exam responses. She was not able to solve basic mathematical operations and did not know in which state Chicago was located. When he asked her if she could name three presidents from the United States, she only named Obama. He also noted she was not dressed appropriately for the situation as she was wearing a T-shirt and sandals.

If you've received training on multiculturalism and cultural sensitivity, you already detected several issues with the student's assumptions about the client and his approach to the case. The client's concerns can probably be analyzed from a multicultural perspective and explained as cultural factors (e.g., wearing sandals, redirecting the tone and content of the session to concerns about family). I would ask you to think of what kind of information the student needed to know to clarify and determine whether his concerns were culturally based or the result of dysfunction that may have needed further attention.

One of the most important things to remember in a clinical interview is not how willing the client is to answer the questions, as this may be completely out of the control of the examiner, but what kind of questions the examiner can ask to establish good rapport, make the client feel comfortable, and increase the likelihood the client will be willing to share information.

To accomplish those goals, it is important to first know which questions to ask. Even if a clinician makes the clients comfortable, the interview will not have clinical value if the information obtained is not relevant to the situation that led the client to seek help. In the following sections, we analyze the clinical interview, including the general areas that are involved, skills to conduct a successful interview, and how these apply to the Mexican American population.

In this chapter, we focus on unstructured clinical interviews, which usually contain open-ended questions and do not have a standardized form of administration (Zimmerman and Mattia, 1999). One advantage of this interview over structured interviews is that the clinician can deviate and take any direction after the client responds to a question, something not always possible in structured interviews.

WHAT IS A CLINICAL INTERVIEW?

Depending on the clinician's training, the setting of the interview, and other factors surrounding the clinical situation, a clinical interview can be viewed differently. For example, a clinical interview conducted in jail to determine if a person is competent to stand trial has a very different purpose than a clinical interview done at a school after a child just revealed he has been a victim of abuse. Yet both will undoubtedly share some characteristics.

A clinical interview is more than a casual conversation. It is an interaction in which a clinician will talk with a client for a specific purpose in order to obtain all the information required to better assist the client. Its main goal is to get information that is consistent, true, and legitimate about the client's situation, specifically the reason the client sought help (Sattler, 2001).

The clinical interview may contain more than one source of information, as it is sometimes necessary to receive collateral information to better help the client. Furthermore, it explores the situation that led the person to get help as well as different aspects of a person's life, such as the way the client behaves in different settings, the way the client feels, how the client communicates and interacts with others, the way the client moves, the client's mental abilities, including memory and intelligence, habits in different settings of the person's life, and the person's perception about the situation (Sattler, 2001).

There are generally two types of clinical interviews. A structured clinical interview usually contains closed-ended questions and is standardized in its administration, which means the instructions are given and the questions are asked in the same way to every person (Groth-Marnat, 2003). We will talk about these interviews in the chapter that explains more in depth psychological assessments and evaluations for Mexican Americans.

COMPONENTS OF A CLINICAL INTERVIEW

As mentioned, a clinical interview is not just a conversation but a way to obtain relevant information about the client in order to develop the most effective treatment plan and to target and address any problems the client may be experiencing. It is important to focus on and explore in detail the situation or conflict for which the person is asking for help. It is also essential, however, to obtain enough information for a general comprehension of the person's personality, his or her past and upbringing, strengths and limitations, and current circumstances, among many other specific areas that can give the clinician a clear picture of how the person behaves beyond the current problem.

The following are some of the most common areas included in a clinical interview (Keatinge and Olin, 1998). There may be others not listed here, and some clinical interviews may not include all of these sections, particularly in different settings.

- Chief complaint
- History of present illness (or present situation)
- Developmental history
- Family history
- Medical history
- Social history
- Educational history
- Psychiatric history
- Previous or current treatment

Keep in mind that exploring some of these areas may feel intrusive to some Mexican Americans. Strategies to engage and make Mexican American clients comfortable have been included in this chapter.

When clinicians refer to the chief complaint, they specifically want to explore the reason the client is being seen by a mental health professional. A person may have more than one chief complaint, and some clients may focus more on medical symptoms than psychological ones. Additionally, some Mexican American clients may not share the chief complaint as a long narrative involving many people and different symptoms and conditions. Remember to be patient when obtaining this information and to sort it out after receiving a clear picture of what may be occurring in a person's life.

The history of present illness includes information about the events that led the client to experience the chief complaint. This section will allow the clinician to get a good picture of potential precipitating factors that led the person to develop the symptoms. As discussed in the previous section, some people may revolve the conversation around other people's actions and situations rather than focusing on themselves.

In the developmental history section, the clinician explores whether the general developmental milestones were met appropriately and whether there were any delays during this process. In this section, the clinician would note, for example, that the client did not start talking or walking until several years after most children (e.g., started walking at age 3, started talking at age 4).

Because of the collectivistic nature of the Mexican American population, some people may include a lot more information in the family history section than what someone experiencing a similar situation but from a different cultural or ethnic group may report. It is appropriate to redirect the conversation if required, but clinicians are strongly encouraged to consider the value of the information not based on their own preconceptions, but on how important the information presented is for the client.

In the medical history section, it is not uncommon for some Mexican American clients to reveal all of the conditions from which they suffer that have been formally diagnosed by a physician, and all that have not been formally diagnosed but that they know they have because someone they trust told them they might. Some clients may also talk about folk medical syndromes or symptoms that are not necessarily part of a medical condition. For example, a few years ago, I assessed a Mexican American woman in her mid-forties presenting with severe anxiety. The purpose of the referral was to educate the client about nonpharmacological methods to cope with anxiety. When I asked about her medical history, she emphasized her anxiety, how she would shake her leg because she was anxious, and the physical symptoms she experienced, such as shortness of breath and trembling. A positive way to address this person without influencing rapport is to obtain all the information while exploring and clarifying things along the way. Even if, as you assess for the reported symptoms, you determine they appear to be directly linked to a psychological condition, the client will feel better if he or she feels heard.

In the social history section of the interview, a person may be asked about social interactions and relationships, substance use history, and what the person does for fun. Two areas that may be sensitive when addressed are sexual activity or sexual orientation and substance use history. Considering that the Mexican American culture still has some embedded prejudice toward sexual minority groups, a Mexican American client may not be willing to disclose this information. Particularly during a first interview while attempting to establish good rapport, it may be better to explore this area through questions related to the person's circumstances, which may reveal something about his or her attitudes. Instead of asking a client about sexual orientation, it may be better to ask how the client gets along with friends and initiate a conversation about the client's romantic relationship history. Clients also may be unsure about disclosing substance abuse information and may not be truthful. It is not unusual to find clients reveal this information in subsequent sessions and not during the first meeting.

Regarding educational history, it is important not only to ask about school performance and the highest grade completed, but also whether the person was in regular classes, special education classes, bilingual classes, and so on.

Psychiatric history and past or current treatments go hand in hand. It is important to know if a person has had previous mental health treatment and to determine whether any of the interventions given were effective. In addition to psychopharmacological treatment, it is important to inquire about a history of counseling or of psychotherapy services in addition to non-Western treatment methods, such as consultations with a folk healer or *curandero* to address any emotional problems.

Because the clinical interview is usually the first step in establishing a therapeutic relationship with the client, it is one of the most important steps in a clinical setting. From the outcome of the clinical interview, the client may feel comfortable enough to engage and participate in a therapeutic relationship with the clinician or feel disillusioned, disconnected, and distant from the therapeutic process, which will lead the person away from services. Considering the negative perception Mexican American clients may have about mental health and mental health treatment, this step is essential in eliminating those fears and making the client feel comfortable. Because of this, it is very important to attempt to use productive and effective skills and interventions.

CLINICAL INTERVIEW SKILLS

Not surprisingly, if the client feels comfortable during the clinical interview, he or she is more likely to share information that will help in the interventions. The following are general behaviors and skills that can help clients feel comfortable during the interview.

Empathy

Being engaged and demonstrating it in the interview is one of the most powerful tools any clinician can use to establish good rapport (Erskine, Moursund, and Trautmann, 1999). Maintaining appropriate eye contact (i.e., not looking away when the person is talking to you), restating what the client says, and showing appropriate emotional nonverbal responses can create an atmosphere that allows the client to feel comfortable enough to share information. Within the Mexican American community, not demonstrating these responses may be viewed as a sign of disrespect and a lack of competence (Aviera, n.d.).

Knowing What to Ask

There are generally two types of interviews that can be utilized in a clinical setting. Structured interviews are those that follow a predetermined order. Their purpose is to stay on task and not to deviate from the topic. One of the disadvantages of these interviews is that they may appear too formal, and the client may not feel as comfortable. They may also prevent a clinician from exploring areas that are not addressed or included in the established format. An unstructured interview refers to an interview that has no predetermined order, allowing the clinician to deviate from format and permitting the exploration of areas that were not included in the interview questions. When offering services to Mexican Americans, unstructured interviews may be more welcomed because they allow for a better rapport (Bernard, 2006). This may be due to this population's preference to engage in conversations that appear to be more fluid. It is important for competent clinicians to be familiar with both approaches and to be flexible and adjust, depending on the client's needs. As we discussed in previous chapters, the Mexican American population can be so diverse that it may not be possible to identify only one of these strategies as the preferred method. However, with information about cultural competency and use of the background and context presented in previous chapters, it is possible for clinicians to be inclined toward one strategy.

Consider two cases: In the first, you are to assess a 9-year-old Mexican American English-speaking male who was referred to you for conduct disorder and behavioral problems, including punching and kicking his parents and siblings, yelling at teachers, and escaping from his classroom at any opportunity. The second case pertains to a 74-year-old Mexican American Spanish-speaking female who was accompanied to the interview by her two daughters because they suspect she is experiencing severe depression and has been refusing to talk to her primary care physician. Which type of interview would you use in these two cases? Would you consider using an unstructured interview with the 9-year-old boy as an attempt to establish good rapport or would it be better to use a structured interview to obtain the necessary information first? In the second case, would it be better to use a structured interview to avoid any possible derailing and rumination as the woman answers the questions, or should you consider utilizing an unstructured interview so there is opportunity to obtain information that may not be on the established questionnaire? While you finish reading the chapter, try to consider these; at the end, you will read more information about these cases.

Know Where You Are Going in This "Dance"

One of the analogies I use to describe an effective clinical interview is a dance. In Mexican American populations, celebrations often include dances. In a way, dance generates rhythm and allows people to find balance while physically interacting with someone else. As one person steps forward, the other person has to step back, and vice versa. If a person steps to the left, the other person has to step to the right, all in synchrony for the dance to be successful. When conducting clinical interviews, it is important to read and detect when to step forward or backward, when to move to the left or to the right, in harmony with the other person. If a client is providing a lot of information that may not be pertinent to the current situation, it is okay to redirect them gently. When working with Mexican American populations, it is important to keep in mind the lack of this "rhythm" may influence the tone of the interview. Consider the following examples.

Luisa is a 63-year-old bilingual Mexican American woman. She sought mental health services due to mild memory problems, feelings of sadness, decreased appetite, and a decreased level of energy. After agreeing to receive services and arriving at the clinic, all the stereotypes, negative perceptions, and stigmas about mental health arise in her mind, preventing her from being very open about the experience. As the clinical interview begins, she is hesitant to talk to the examiner. To establish good rapport, the clinician starts to ask questions unrelated to what brought her to get help. Instead of directly asking about the symptoms or the potential causes, he asks her to share some information about her grandchildren and her childhood. Luisa first appears guarded and responds with only short answers. However, the clinician notices a smile on Luisa's face after sharing the time her youngest granddaughter prepared a fashion show with her favorite teddy bears and toys as the audience. The clinician sees Luisa's response as positive and considers it advantageous to the interview. The clinician asks more about the event, which motivates Luisa to elaborate more about her granddaughters and about a very intimate and private part of her life, her family. With skill, strategies, and a sensitivity to "dance" during the interview, the clinician moved back or forward, depending on the tone of the conversation, and he eventually made Luisa forget about her negative perceptions about mental health. Suddenly, the experience was not as formal or negative as she had anticipated. Instead, it became a pleasant conversation about her grandchildren.

A key strategy in this example is not only the questions the clinician asked, but also having Luisa talk and engaging her in a clinical interview without her noticing. By talking about her family and specifically her grandchildren, her defenses and cognitive resistances were lifted, allowing the clinician to explore the problem in depth while creating and establishing good rapport.

Be Careful with the Client's Perspective of You

This strategy is suggested not because the clinician may belittle the client, but because the client, based on his or her level of acculturation and other social factors, may be very sensitive about the clinician and may feel belittled even if the clinician did nothing wrong. It is particularly important to be aware of nonverbal gestures and reactions. Language may cause people to misunderstand messages. We will offer more information about the use of translators in the next chapter. However, keep in mind that, as discussed in Chapter 6, communication is mostly transmitted through nonverbal gestures and means. It is possible to reduce the likelihood that a client may perceive a clinician in a threatening or unpleasant manner. General rules include being aware of the clinician's speech characteristics. It is best to utilize verbalization with appropriate tone, volume, and rate, and to use neutral and nonverbal gestures. In some cases, Mexican American clients may feel more comfortable if there is no desk between the client and the clinician (Sue and Sue, 2012).

Several years ago, I worked with a client who was very sensitive to these issues and shared that she was very offended when a previous therapist talked to her with a louder and slower speech pattern because she did not understand a question the clinician had asked. This reaction made her feel ignorant and that there was something wrong with her. The therapist's intention may have been to communicate in the easiest way possible, but it affected the therapeutic relationship.

MENTAL STATUS EXAM

The Mental Status Exam is one of the most important components of a clinical interview. Its purpose is to assess abilities and characteristics of a client in order to assist in determining areas that may need to be treated. Some standardized instruments measure the mental status of an individual, as do informal methods.

Some components of this exam are based on self-reporting, relying on the accuracy of the responses based on the person's perceptions; other components are not based on what the person perceives, but on what the clinician can observe.

An example of self-reported information is expressing feelings of sadness. People may have a general idea of what a person means when he or she feels sad (e.g., has crying spells, feels lonely and worthless); the personal experience of feeling sad is subjective and based on the individual's characteristics, experiences, and perceptions. If someone reports feeling sad, he or she may not really mean what other people mean when they say they feel sad, but we can assume the person has a general feeling of not being well, and we take that report as a piece of information of the Mental Status Exam.

An example of what the clinician may observe rather than what the client reports is the behavior during the assessment. The client may not admit behaving restlessly. The clinician, however, may note the person paced constantly, appeared to be fidgety, and was constantly moving his or her legs. These observations can serve as a very important tool to clarify information and to determine what would be the best plan of action for every client.

Common Components of the Mental Status Exam

Let us take a few steps back and consider the information usually included in the Mental Status Exam. As mentioned, some of these areas are explored by asking the client questions, while others are simply based on the clinician's observations (Groth-Marnat, 2003).

Attention and concentration: Because several conditions can generate deficits and impairment in attention and concentration, it is important to assess these during the Mental Status Exam and as part of a clinical interview. In essence, this area is evaluated by determining the extent to which a client is able to maintain focus on mental tasks.

Judgment: The client may be asked how he or she would behave under an unusual situation or circumstance that may require decisions to solve the problem. Particularly when working with Mexican Americans, this question requires sensitivity to the culture's characteristics. For example, a person may express not wanting to contact law enforcement officials if a crime was committed against a neighbor if the person is undocumented and afraid of being deported.

Insight: Insight refers to the extent to which the client has knowledge and is aware of his or her own difficulties and the ability and responsibility to solve the difficulties, including treatment. Insight also may be influenced by cultural factors. For example, a person who suffers from depression and is particularly affected by neurovegetative symptoms (appetite, sleep, and energy problems), which are commonly treated with antidepressants, opposes receiving medication due to social and cultural stigmas; that person may be perceived as someone with poor insight who refuses to accept the need for treatment of any kind.

Mood: Mood is always a subjective area that consists of how the client is generally feeling at the time of the assessment. It is common to put in quotes how the client describes his or her mood. Caution is urged toward clinicians analyzing the words used by the client, as some words may not intend to reflect what we understand them to convey.

Affect: If mood is the client's description of how he or she feels, affect is the way he or she appears. Instead of using a subjective report, we are able to describe how the client appears. Affect together with mood are two areas to carefully assess in clinical settings, particularly in understanding the severity of a client's condition or whether a client is authentic and genuine with his or her report of symptoms or appears untruthful. For example, a person may minimize the impact of symptoms by reporting that his or her mood is "fine" while having a very negative and sad affect, suggesting the person is not really fine and may be experiencing symptoms of depression. Additionally, if a person is exaggerating symptoms or reporting symptoms he or she is not really experiencing, you would expect to see inconsistencies between the person's mood and affect.

Memory: There are different ways to assess memory functioning. To begin with, it is important to understand that different types of memory exist. For the purpose of the Mental Status Exam, it is uncommon for clinicians to assess the most basic and quick type of memory, which is known as sensory memory, or the information obtained through the senses and stored for only a few seconds. From there, the information is either transferred to short-term memory or discarded. Short-term memory usually lasts about 30 seconds and is limited in capacity. After 30 seconds, the information is discarded or transferred to long-term memory. Working memory, which can also be assessed through the Mental Status Exam, is the person's ability to not only retain information but to manage and manipulate it. Long-term memory can be divided into two major sections: recent and remote. Recent memory is usually information that has been stored for the past two years and that, although not available at all times, can be retrieved whenever requested. Remote memory is the section of long-term memory that has been stored longer than two years and is usually the most resistant to decay. For example, if I asked you to think about what you were doing on the morning of September 11, 2001, you are likely to remember because the date and the events that occurred then were significant and were stored.

Orientation: Clients are usually assessed to determine if they are aware of where they are, who they are, the date and time of the day, and the situation. A person with different types of conditions such as psychosis, dementia, or delirium may not be oriented.

Attitude: This area focuses on the client's attitude during the assessment. A person may be cooperative or uncooperative, negative, guarded, or evasive.

Thought process: In this section, clinicians often explore areas that may indicate a psychotic or thought disorder. Clients may be asked if they experience any types of hallucinations, if they suffer from delusional thinking, and if they have an abstract or concrete way of thinking. The clinician also notes whether the client shows loss of associations or displays circumstantial, tangential, or referential thinking, and documents whether the person's behaviors were consistent with his or her responses. For example, just because a client denies experiencing auditory or visual hallucinations does not mean that he or she does not experience them. The person's behavior can also reveal them. A client's response to internal stimuli or to stimuli that the clinician may not perceive should be noted in this section. That information should assist the clinician in formulating the case, determining the main problems, and developing the most effective treatment plan.

Thought content: This area explores the thoughts the person has in relation to symptoms or problems. The clinician usually documents in this section if there are any obsessions, compulsions, or reported phobias, if the client has suicidal ideation, or if the client has homicidal ideation (Groth-Marnat, 2003).

Behavior during the interview and assessment: This section is particularly important when there is a suspicion that the client is not completely honest (exaggerating symptoms or minimizing the problems he or she is experiencing as a result of the symptoms). This area is also always useful for other reasons. Therapeutically speaking, a client's behavior reflects the client's thoughts and feelings about a topic. Thus, monitoring and being sensitive to the client's behavior is a very powerful tool when offering counseling or psychotherapy services, which we will explore more in depth in the following chapter.

Appearance: This section includes how the person looks, how he or she is dressed, and general physical characteristics. For example, a clinician may describe that a person looks older than his or her stated age, that he or she is somewhat disheveled, and that he or she is wearing blue jeans and a Green Bay Packers jersey.

Speech, language: It is important to document the characteristics of speech, usually by noting the tone, volume, and rate. Language is a very important area to document, especially with the Mexican American population. Keeping in mind that not every Mexican American will speak Spanish at all or as a first language, the clinician needs to determine which is the primary language so the Mental Status Exam can provide as much and as accurate information as possible. Some people consider themselves bilingual but do not necessarily understand Spanish without mixing words in English (Spanglish). One way to ensure the person can be assessed in his or her primary language is to ask what language is spoken in the home. In some cases, Mexican American clients may speak both languages at very similar or the same level. If this is the case, it is appropriate to ask which language they prefer, and if they say either, the clinician can suggest one.

Caution About Translation and Descriptors

Several years ago, I visited a graduate program that specialized in mental health treatment. I was privileged to observe their process of offering counseling services from the beginning until the end. One client was a 15-year-old Mexican American male who was referred for services by his mother because, according to her, he had been acting *curioso.* This term can be literally translated as *curious.* When the client's mother described what she meant, however she stated that he had been acting strange recently and had been increasingly isolative and irritable.

When clients use some words in Spanish or if they literally translate some words into English, it is important to be mindful of the meaning they give those words as some may be used differently from their English definition. Whether utilizing a translator or if the clinician speaks Spanish, it is important to not assume the meaning of some of these words and to clarify with the clients any words that may not be as clear. Here are a few examples of words that may be misused or misunderstood to describe a person's characteristics:

If clients say they feel *curioso (or curiosa),* which can be literally translated as curious, the client may be referring to a strange, funny, or unusual presentation. Usually, people offering collateral information will describe someone this way.

Some clients utilize the word *desesperado* (desperate). It is common for people to mean they feel anxious, restless, or overwhelmed, and that these feelings are accompanied by a hyperactive presentation. Some clients may also use the words *ansioso* or *nervioso* to describe these same symptoms. Keep in mind that when clients use those terms, they may be referring to hyperactivity and impulse control rather than anxiety. It is very important that clinicians clarify this information whenever it is presented to them.

The Data Obtained from the Clinical Interview

Once information is obtained through a clinical interview and a Mental Status Exam, what can we do with it? What should we do with it? I always remind my students of a couple of rules. The first is that we only make clinical decisions based on the available data. If the data are not consistent with a certain diagnosis, we do not assign the data to the person. In contrast, even if the person does not want to accept the presence of a certain type of pathology, if the data support it, then it is the clinician's responsibility to provide that information to the client, keeping in mind sensitivity and coping strategies to prepare clients for the aftermath.

One of the best tools we can get from the application and implementation of a Mental Status Exam is how the data vary and how they are consistent or inconsistent with the rest of the information. Consider the following example:

Juan is an 18-year-old Hispanic, English-speaking male who has been diagnosed with Borderline Personality Disorder. He was referred for individual psychotherapy because his family was concerned he would hurt himself, something he had threatened for the past two years. He appeared to have superficial lacerations in both of his arms and reported feeling very sad and angry. During the clinical interview with the Mental Status Exam, however, his affect and presentation were not consistent with what he was reporting. For example, whenever reporting that he had experienced thoughts of suicide, he would laugh and his affect would not demonstrate any negativity. He also shared that he had experienced thoughts of wanting to die because his girlfriend left him. While reporting this information, however, his affect would not change. Also, during a very intense section of the interview in which the client disclosed he had been a victim of sexual abuse, his affect was bright and he constantly smiled.

There may be a wide variety of reasons why Juan smiled or had a bright affect while reporting serious incidents in his life. At this point and with only the information presented, it would not be possible to determine whether Juan was lying about his symptoms, but it can certainly be a hypothesis that may need further exploration. Some people smile as a defense mechanism to cover true emotions about something very disturbing they experienced. This may be one of those cases. But it's possible either the symptoms or the experiences he was reporting were not accurate. As a clinician, it is important to first obtain all the necessary information to determine what would be the next most appropriate step to take.

Conclusion

Remember the two cases you read about in a previous section of this chapter? The first was about a 9-year-old Mexican American English-speaking male referred to address conduct disorder and behavioral problems, and the second was about a 74-year-old Mexican American Spanish-speaking female who was referred due to potential severe depression. There are a couple of things I would like to address about these cases. What type or style of interview should be utilized to gather clinical information? Which type would be most effective: structured or unstructured interviews? The answer I can provide (and I hope I do not disappoint anyone with this response) is that it depends. In general terms, when interviewing children, it may be more convenient and productive to utilize unstructured interviews, as these are more likely to make children comfortable and willing to share information (Sattler, 2001). However, there are some instances in which it may be more useful to use a structured interview with children, such as when exploring specific symptoms of mental illness (Sattler, 2001). In the second case, it may be more useful to utilize a structured interview to make sure the client stays on task and answers all the questions with relevant information. This format may affect rapport, however, and it may be more useful to maintaining an appropriate therapeutic relationship to utilize an unstructured interview. Again, this choice depends on several factors. The key in choosing the interview and the style to use is to be sensitive and receptive to the characteristics and needs of the client. From the analogy I used earlier to compare a clinical interview with a dance, I would say the most important thing is to engage and fall into the rhythm of the dance. Once this occurs, you can determine which interview would be most useful for the client.

Consider the information presented in this chapter not as absolute truth or an ultimate guide to follow in every case. Instead, I recommend the information be used as a supplement to clinical skills you may already have. By engaging and becoming more sensitive to the needs of Mexican American clients, it is possible to make more appropriate and effective decisions that can change the trajectory of the therapeutic alliance and relationship. Doing this can also increase the effectiveness of the treatment and change the general perception about mental health in the Mexican American population.

SUMMARY

In this chapter, we discussed the clinical interview process and reviewed information that may be useful when working with Mexican American clients. Even though the theme and tone of this chapter and the rest of the book is to encourage clinicians to become more culturally sensitive to this population, it is also important to go over some skills, strategies, and potential difficulties when attempting to conduct an accurate clinical interview.

Two major areas of this chapter are the section describing the characteristics of a clinical interview and the section reviewing elements included in a Mental Status Exam. In each of these sections, there is important information offered about the Mexican American population and their perceptions about these processes. Because the clinical interview is usually the first contact a clinician has with a client, it is particularly important to be aware of potential obstacles in the clinical interview in order to reduce their impact and to promote and engage the client in a healthy therapeutic relationship by establishing good rapport. The information given in this chapter also serves as the precursor to Chapter 9, which contains information about offering counseling and psychotherapy services to the Mexican American population.

Chapter 9

Counseling Mexican Americans

A few years ago, I attended a conference focused on how to competently offer multicultural psychological and counseling services. In one session, there were several representatives from programs that promoted diversity and immersion in Mexican culture. Their programs consisted of sending students to different parts of Mexico to live for several months. The goal was for students to learn not only how to speak Spanish, but for them to understand aspects of Mexican culture, including foods, the daily struggles Mexicans may encounter, and other characteristics that can only be attained by experiencing them. One thing that can help reduce discrimination toward any group is the level of dominant society immersion: The higher the level, the lower the potential discrimination (Awad, 2010).

As conference speakers presented these topics, an audience member asked about the use of translators in sessions, particularly their use in psychotherapy or counseling sessions, and how to reduce any issues that may arise as a result. Each presenter was given an opportunity to answer, and although the first presenters said their programs did not cover this issue, they explained that other programs may discuss the impact. When the last presenter's turn came, he simply said translators should not be used and clinicians should speak Spanish if the clients spoke Spanish. There was a moment of silence, and the audience seemed perplexed by this response. According to his view, clinicians who do not speak Spanish should not offer these services to Spanish-speaking clients.

Why am I sharing this story at the beginning of this chapter that discusses the offering of counseling and psychotherapy services to the Mexican American population? Please consider all of the elements we have discussed in previous chapters and the characteristics of the Mexican American population. Even though a large number of Mexican Americans speak English, several Mexican Americans only speak Spanish. As we stated in Chapter 6, the language of Mexican Americans can be very diverse, and just because a clinician speaks "standard" Spanish, he or she may not necessarily be able to communicate effectively in counseling or psychotherapy sessions. Knowing the language can be as important as knowing or understanding the person's culture.

Do I believe translators should never be used? Or should always be used? The answer to both questions is no. The answer depends on several other factors beyond language, including cultural sensitivity and competency. However, it is important for clinicians to be aware of their own limitations and to determine whether they are culturally prepared to offer services under these circumstances.

GENERAL MULTICULTURAL PRACTICES

Even though there has been increased interest in exploring the role of cultural factors on development, personality, psychopathology, and mental health in general, a lot of unanswered questions remain. Nowadays, graduate psychology programs offer multicultural counseling courses, and they usually require at least one of these courses to be completed prior to graduating. Furthermore, licensing boards now require a minimum number of continuing education courses that present multicultural issues. Considering the complexity of culture and cultural influences, however, these requirements are not necessarily enough for a person to become culturally competent.

A key recommendation about multicultural counseling is that clinicians first become aware of their own biases (Sue and Sue, 2012). The question is not whether clinicians have biases but the extent to which these influence the counseling or therapeutic process without the clinician being aware. Without accepting that every person has biases, it is not possible to become aware of the role of the clinician's own preferences and perceptions during the session.

Considering the significant power difference between the client and the clinician in a therapeutic relationship, it is important to know how the clinician's perceptions may influence the client in a negative way according to the client's cultural background. Even with the clinician's best intentions, a risk exists that, if the clinician is not aware of the power differential and cultural differences, the path of therapy may not be in the best interest of the client. Consider the following example:

Paula is a 36-year-old English-speaking Mexican American female who was referred for counseling services by her family doctor after she admitted suffering from the following symptoms of depression: feelings of sadness, decreased appetite, lack of energy and motivation, and thoughts of worthlessness. Her therapist was a middle-aged white Caucasian male who had been in practice for several years. During the session, Paula revealed she was depressed because she recently broke up with her boyfriend after she found out he was unfaithful. Her therapist placed more emphasis, however, on the fact that Paula continued to live with her family and believed she suffered from Dependent Personality Disorder. Through the sessions, Paula's therapist focused on assisting Paula in what he called "gaining your independence," which consisted of Paula being able to move out of her family's house and live independently.

The therapist was probably genuinely attempting to help Paula with his intervention. However, there are a few things to consider: It is possible Paula did not suffer from a Dependent Personality Disorder and that what the therapist considered to be pathological (i.e., living with her family at age 36) may have been greatly influenced by cultural factors. This does not mean all Mexican Americans would prefer to live with their families until middle adulthood. The point is that clinicians need to have an open mind and to view things from more than their own perspective.

SOME FACTORS THAT CAN INFLUENCE COUNSELING/PSYCHOTHERAPY

As mentioned in previous sections, a wide variety of factors can influence the counseling or therapeutic relationship between a Mexican American client and a clinician. The goal of becoming a culturally competent provider is not to know everything about a culture or to adapt the practices of the other culture as the clinician's own. It is to encourage clinicians to become aware of the fact that there may be significant cultural differences and, therefore, important differences regarding how each party perceives the world. A major problem that emerges is the complexity of what culture is and the numerous factors that play a role in each person's life. From this perspective, culture is not only an ethnic group, but also many other characteristics that dictate a person's behavior. An example of one characteristic is level of socioeconomic status. People from different socioeconomic statuses are likely to perceive the world very differently, even if they share a cultural background such as being Mexican American.

Racism, Prejudice, and Discrimination

Some of the most difficult social obstacles Mexican Americans have to contend with are discrimination, prejudice, and racism. These obstacles may not be the same for every Mexican American in the United States as some reside in more diverse locations and some may even live where the majority is of Mexican descent. Yet, these concepts can be very significant when considering the development and social perception of individuals.

Discrimination and prejudice may be commonly perceived as something done purposefully, but this is not always the case. To deepen the analysis of these social concepts in the Mexican American population, it is important to first distinguish and define each. According to the Merriam-Webster dictionary website, discrimination is defined as "the practice of unfairly treating a person or group of people differently from other people or groups of people." Prejudice is "an unfair feeling of dislike for a person or group because of race, sex, religion, etc." and "a feeling of like or dislike for someone or something especially when it is not reasonable or logical." Racism is "a belief that race is the primary determinant of human traits and capacities and that racial differences produce an inherent superiority of a particular race." This concept is "racial prejudice or discrimination."

To summarize and compare and contrast these definitions, it is safe to say that discrimination is the action or behavior toward a person or group that is being treated differently from others whereas prejudice is the attitude or feeling of dislike of any given person or group due to race, sex, religion, or other factors. However, prejudice does not necessarily involve behaving in an unfavorable manner toward a specific group. Racism is a concept in which people may feel one race is better than another, and it can lead to discrimination and prejudice based solely on race.

Does this mean that people are always aware of their own biases and perceptions? Even though prejudice means having a conscious dislike of a person or group, it is also possible to have imbedded preconceptions about certain groups that we may view as normal and standard when that group may find those preconceptions offensive.

There is another term that has come to revolutionize the way multiculturalism is perceived. In 2007, Sue, Capodilupo, Torino, Bucceri, Holder, Nadal, and Esquilin published an article that went beyond what people knew about discrimination and racism (Sue *et al.*, 2007). I had the opportunity of attending a lecture by Dr. Sue a few years ago, and he explained how the content of the article was based on ideas proposed by African-American psychologists in the 1970s. During that talk, many of his colleagues also shared the experiences they had after the article was published. Minority groups felt the information included there was very significant and contributed to the better understanding of minority groups and how to properly address these issues in clinical settings. Some groups not only were not in agreement with the information presented, however, but also considered it to be against white Caucasians. The concept he proposed from that article is what he called racial microaggressions, which can be defined as "subtle, stunning, often automatic, and non-verbal exchanges which are 'put downs'" (Pierce, Carew, Pierce-Gonzalez, and Willis, 1978). These microaggressions can be verbal and may not be conscious; the person may not be aware he or she is doing it (Sue *et al.*, 2007).

Because microaggressions can be unconscious and may occur without intent, it is especially important to understand this concept prior to offering counseling or psychotherapy services to Mexican Americans. One of the best ways to achieve this understanding begins with a deep, detailed, and complete analysis of oneself, including an exploration of personal biases and predisposed concepts that may drive our behavior. Not understanding this may give clinicians the misconception they are culturally sensitive and competent to offer services to minority groups, which can assist in masking those beliefs and attitudes and lead to the emergence of microaggressions. Microaggressions can be both conscious or unconscious, but those that come without the awareness of the person can be more harmful to clients in clinical settings. The clinician may not be aware of the impact of his or her beliefs and behaviors, which can significantly affect the therapeutic process (Sue *et al.*, 2007). The following is an example of a microaggression. Note that for a microaggression to exist, it does not need to include ill intention.

While I was working on my thesis prior to obtaining my first master's degree, I inquired about employment at a school district office. At that time, I had long, loose hair, and my beard was somewhat long (about half an inch). I was wearing jeans and a T-shirt, and as I walked into the office I asked the receptionist where the job applications were located. She said the employment applications for professional positions were found on the left side, but the ones I probably was looking for, which were for paraprofessional positions, were found on the right side. She smiled after sharing this information, demonstrating a strong conviction that she had helped someone who was confused. Because of the way I looked, the receptionist probably assumed I did not have a degree and was looking for a paraprofessional position. She appeared to have the full intention of helping me, but it did not cross her mind that I had an undergraduate degree and was about to obtain a master's degree.

Personal biases and even unconscious processes can be very influential in a counseling or psychotherapy session. Sometimes, they can affect the client without the awareness of the clinician.

Consider the following example: An older white Caucasian therapist worked with clients from different ethnic groups. He considered himself a multicultural and culturally sensitive clinician, prepared to work with different groups because he had experience working with people of Asian, African, and Native American descent. However, he had never worked with clients of Latino descent. When a Mexican American client came to his office, he assumed that he was culturally competent to offer services to this population as well. As the session moved on, he was aware of the collectivistic nature of this group, the potential language differences, and the sociocultural and economical adversity this group may encounter compared with people from other groups. The problem came when the client revealed he was undocumented. The therapist, having been raised in a conservative family and active in the Republican Party, did not perceive the client in the same way as he initially had, and the tone of the session was driven toward issues and aspects related to the client's undocumented status. The therapist worked with the client for several sessions before the client stopped attending.

The therapist may have talked about issues that probably were not the most important for the client at that moment, and his focus was significantly influenced by his own perceptions. Not being aware of his own biases about undocumented immigrants made him believe he was competent to offer therapeutic services to people from different minority groups, but that was not quite accurate.

Exploring Own Biases

Several years ago, I attended a conference that did not focus on clinical topics, but addressed a wide variety of issues related to social disparity. I was very impressed by one of the speakers who talked about the process he went through when he found out he had implicit and, to an extent, unconscious predisposed biases and discrimination. He said that while speaking to a large group at a professional conference, an audience member confronted him with the idea that he may be biased and therefore may have had prejudice and shown discriminatory behavior toward others. The speaker said he first argued with the audience member and felt offended. After thinking about it for several days, however, he realized he had been partial and biased and that he had been implicitly discriminatory against people with certain characteristics. While sharing this information, the speaker began to cry, showing the high levels of emotion he felt when exploring this behavior. I share this example because some people avoid exploring their personal biases since it can be difficult to contend with what they may find.

"Accurate" Paranoia

It is not uncommon for Mexican American clients or patients to have a certain level of skepticism about the health care system. As mentioned in previous chapters, acculturation is negatively correlated with mental health; the more acculturated a person is to the United States, the more mental health problems that develop. Furthermore, in the health care system there can be negative perceptions about immigrants and discrimination and prejudice against Mexican Americans. When referring to paranoia as "accurate," I do not mean that paranoia as a symptom is real. Instead, it is important when working with Mexican Americans that we consider their worldview. Just as with other groups, we have to consider that their issues or perceptions may not be a distortion; that they may be true representations of their reality. For example, imagine a client seeks individual psychotherapy or counseling because of feelings of being treated differently from others due to his or her accent. Perhaps a cognitive distortion makes the client feel inadequate and singled out, but it is possible people are actually making fun of his or her accent.

THE COUNSELING/PSYCHOTHERAPEUTIC PROCESS

The information in previous chapters should be considered as a context when working with Mexican American clients. Not every client would fit all characteristics or descriptors in this book, but this information can help while forming the clinical picture of the individual. Because the counseling and psychotherapy techniques must be appropriate to the client's situation, characteristics, and abilities, the clinician must conduct a thorough clinical interview prior to proposing a treatment plan or techniques to address the chief complaint.

Language

As mentioned (see also Chapter 6), language is a significant factor that can assist or impair the therapeutic relationship. Even though a large number of Mexican Americans speak Spanish, it is important to not assume everyone does. Because language is one of the most commonly used parameters to determine a person's level of acculturation, determining this variable can determine the level of acculturation.

Ideally, the clinician would speak the same language as the client. Unfortunately, this is not always possible. If a translator is needed, caution is strongly urged in communicating. The message may rely more on the context than the actual words. Using a high-context form of communication while expressing information through a translator may convey the idea, particularly because the Mexican American population generally uses a high-context form of communication.

Another important factor to consider is that the translator may not be as well-versed in technical or clinical terms, so it may be difficult to literally translate some ideas. To facilitate communicating any idea, it would be easier for the clinician to express, in English, any information in the simplest terms possible.

Clinicians who speak Spanish must keep in mind that there are different types of Spanish and that some words may mean different things for different cultures and people. This is particularly important when assessing the client's progress and offering recommendations and interventions.

Cultural Factors

In addition to language, cultural factors, such as the involvement of family in a person's life, can influence the way the treatment plan is delineated. Some people may want to involve their family in their recovery process. Clinicians may prefer to not involve the family for confidentiality considerations, but some clients may not feel as comfortable or as willing to work without family involvement.

Clients who suffer from more severe psychopathologies such as a Major Depressive Disorder or some symptoms of psychosis may have a particularly difficult time accepting their condition and may want to justify it with culture-bound conditions. I have seen several clients who, after significant weight loss from decreased appetite during a major depressive episode, believe they are victims of a curse or of witchcraft. Sometimes the clients engage cultural practices to address the symptoms, such as a *barrida* or the drinking of traditional teas. As culturally competent clinicians, it is important to validate their preference and attempt to incorporate such practices into their recovery process as much as possible while offering psychoeducational sessions to explain the nature of the condition and the role of mental health treatment in addressing such symptoms.

Family Involvement

Particularly in children and adolescents, family involvement can be crucial to the success of any mental health intervention. The best and most effective approach to offering therapeutic interventions to children involves a collaborative approach. Family members and parents may not always feel heard and may feel discouraged by clinical or supportive services. Culturally speaking, Mexican American families may consider the best intervention includes group cohesiveness, integration, cooperation among the responsible parties, and interdependence (Santiago-Rivera, 2003; Dotson-Blake, 2010). United States society may consider the most effective interventions, however, to be those that rely on autonomy and independence (Santiago-Rivera, 2003). These differences in approaches can cause significant despair and discouragement in people whose needs may not be properly culturally addressed and can have negative consequences in the client's life.

For example, a young Mexican American undocumented immigrant was a victim of bullying at school. Unable to resolve the conflict after attempting to get assistance from the child's teacher, her parents decided to send her back to Mexico to live with a family member where they thought she could achieve quality academic instruction without being emotionally abused. The child's father believed the bullying continued and his daughter did not get any help because they were undocumented, so he decided to speak with the school counselor for guidance in dealing with the distress the situation brought to his family (Santiago-Rivera, 2003).

The child's parents believed sending their daughter to live in Mexico with a family member was the best option. Had they received assistance from the teacher or school counselor to begin with, the situation could have ended differently. In addition to the child's constant exposure to bullying, the father was also concerned about the lack of support from his daughter's teacher. Not feeling heard and feeling that their undocumented status played a role in the lack of support for his daughter led the parents to believe that the only option to resolve the conflict was to send their daughter away.

Another example in which family may play an important role in the therapeutic process is dealing with vocational issues. A humanistic approach and interventions from Positive Psychology can be useful when setting vocational outcome expectations for Mexican American adolescents. However, family involvement is also strongly recommended. Parents should receive training and information through workshops in order to be aware of their role in motivating and supporting adolescents while setting vocational expectations. It is also recommended that parents be engaged in their children's academic career and for practitioners to offer effective services in Spanish when needed (Cavazos Vela, Lenz, Sparrow, Gonzalez, and Hinojosa, 2015). It is not unusual for clinicians to assume family members know information when it has never been transmitted or explained to them. By considering these interventions, transmitting useful and necessary information can make a difference in the child's life.

Family involvement can be a crucial asset in the success of behavioral change when identifying substance abuse and proposed interventions. In some cases, appropriate treatment does not occur due to a lack of family involvement (Gragg and Wilson, 2011). Particularly when working with adolescent Mexican Americans who have substance use disorders, family involvement can increase the probability of success and can be achieved using a variety of multirelational processes. Because Mexican American cultural norms can keep people from speaking to strangers about personal problems, it is important for the therapist to be approachable and to promote family involvement in treatment, even if it goes against social prescriptions. Furthermore, it is important for Mexican American families to have the opportunity to share stories either to the clinician or to other families in group counseling or therapy. One reason Mexican Americans may not be willing to be as open in therapy is fear of being criticized or judged, which may be driven by the negative connotation of mental illness within this population. Lastly, it is important for the clinician to communicate cultural competency with the suggestions at the beginning of this chapter and to make the clients feel understood and heard. Otherwise, they may not want to continue receiving services (Gragg and Wilson, 2011).

COUNSELING/PSYCHOTHERAPY TECHNIQUES

I would like to share a conversation I had with a physician who works at the hospital where I offer psychological services. Prior to this position, he owned a medical clinic that served primarily migrant workers of Mexican descent. One of the first times he saw a patient in this clinic, he was overwhelmed hearing the problems and distress the patient was experiencing due to family issues. The physician felt somewhat sad and uncomfortable with the idea that, even though he heard all of the patient's problems, the solution was not within his reach. He also was concerned about how the patient would react when she learned he could not do anything about the issues. To his surprise, during the patient's follow-up appointment, she expressed gratitude and did not appear to be affected by the fact that he was not able to fix her problems. He learned that his patients did not want anyone to solve their problems; they just wanted someone to hear them. Being culturally sensitive can facilitate an optimal level of trust and engagement, allowing the clinician and the client to establish an appropriate and effective therapeutic relationship.

As with other groups, there are general techniques of counseling and psychotherapy that have been shown to be effective for the Mexican American population, even without any special modification to adjust to this particular group. Some attempts to modify interventions to be culturally specific for Mexican Americans did not yield significant improvement compared with interventions offered without modification. Culturally sensitive skills, however, can significantly improve the outcome of the therapeutic intervention and can be more important than modifying an intervention (McCabe and Yeh, 2009). The results of one case in which a Parent–Child Interaction Therapy curriculum was modified according to the characteristics of Mexican American clients (which the authors called *Guiando a Niños Activos* or GANA) was not significantly different from the traditional, nonmodified Parent–Child Interaction Therapy (McCabe and Yeh, 2009). This result does not mean other modifications would not work, but that even without modified curriculums or established interventions, it is possible to offer quality, culturally competent therapeutic and counseling services by following the recommendations in this chapter. The following are just a few examples of techniques and their impact on the Mexican American population. These should be used as the basis for developing culturally sensitive approaches and should not be viewed as the only acceptable interventions.

Active Listening

This skill is the use of verbal and nonverbal behavior that promotes reassurance and confidence that the clinician is attentive and engaged in the information presented by the client (Hill, 2009). This skill may help resolve potential difficulties caused by social constraints such as discrimination or prejudice that could impair a therapeutic intervention for the Mexican American population. By restating, showing attentive nonverbal behaviors, and displaying empathy throughout a counseling or psychotherapy session, the client can feel more engaged and comfortable, and any cultural factor that could affect the therapeutic relationship would dissipate.

Groups

There are several advantages to group counseling or psychotherapy instead of individual sessions. A clinician can reach out to several people at once, and the skills and abilities that require a person's involvement may be facilitated if a client feels supported by others with similar circumstances. Some Mexican Americans may be hesitant to speak up and offer their own opinions if they feel the group could be antagonistic due to cultural, social, ethnic, or socioeconomic factors. If these issues are addressed, groups can be a very important tool, particularly if offering activities that promote collaboration and incorporate culturally relevant conversations. Mexican Americans may feel more comfortable engaging in and being part of this type of intervention (Malott and Paone, 2013).

Cuento Therapy

When working with Mexican American children, *cuento* therapy has shown to be useful. This type of intervention consists of sharing a culturally appropriate story that ends with a moral message, promoting the emotional growth of the child (Villalba, Ivers, and Ohlms, 2010). *Cuento* literally means "story" or "tale," but unlike other interventions that only consist of sharing a story with children, the stories shared during *cuento* therapy include culturally relevant elements that allow the Mexican American child to identify with the story's components.

Spiritual–Cultural Approaches

Interest in exploring new and effective clinical frameworks for minority groups, including Mexican Americans, has grown, but there is still a great need to expand on the factors that can create culturally appropriate interventions. Some of these factors have to do with spiritual and cultural beliefs. Spirituality is undoubtedly embedded in Mexican American culture. As presented in Chapter 2, religion and spiritual beliefs have been a constant variable in historical and contemporary Mexican and Mexican American cultures. One of the most important things to keep in mind when becoming a culturally competent clinician is the person's perception about spirituality and cultural beliefs in his or her own treatment. Some may feel more comfortable with their mental health treatment if their folk healer plays a role. If so, should the clinician permit this request? In what capacity should this be allowed? The answer to this is, as with other questions, it depends. If the folk healer can affect the therapeutic relationship and hinder the person's recovery, then it would be better to exclude him or her from treatment while explaining to the client the basis for the decision. I asked the physician who owned a migrant clinic about this, and he said if the treatment and involvement does not affect the clinical treatment that is evidence-based and supported by research, then he included the folk healer.

In order to integrate cultural healing practices into the counseling or psychotherapy process, it is important to understand some of their similarities.

This issue can become complicated. Consider the following example: A client diagnosed with cancer is receiving chemotherapy. After his second treatment, he informs a clinician he wants to stop the treatment because he would like to be healed by a folk healer only. At this point, what would be the role of the clinician? Would it be culturally sensitive to encourage the client to continue receiving chemotherapy? Are we certain the treatment given by the folk healer will be ineffective? These questions may not have a single answer. Being culturally competent does not mean ignoring other knowledge that is clear and well known by practitioners. If the clinician explains to the client that the treatment offered by Western medicine is research based, he or she can still be culturally competent. The first step is to inform the client thoroughly about the potential consequences of the decision, basing it on research and information from the body of knowledge of the field. The focus should not be to diminish the importance of the client's cultural beliefs, but to give the client all the necessary information to make an informed decision.

Language, Competency, and Code Switching during Mexican American Counseling and Psychotherapy

As mentioned in this book, several issues can hinder the effective therapeutic relationships between clinicians and Mexican American clients. Language is one of these. Research has shown that ethnicity of the clinician may not be as important a factor as other variables, and that bilingual Caucasian clinicians are considered as competent as Mexican American bilingual clinicians, if not more so (Ramos-Sánchez, 2009). Mexican American clients may feel comfortable with clinicians who speak both English and Spanish, even if the client speaks both, and not only Spanish. This is significantly more favorable if the clinician is Euro-American, suggesting that if all clinicians who work with Mexican Americans are able to express themselves with a mixture of English and Spanish when appropriate and culturally relevant, the clients are more likely to open up and express more emotions than when working with monolingual English-speaking clinicians (Ramos-Sánchez, 2007).

SUMMARY

In this chapter, we discuss counseling and psychotherapy interventions for Mexican American clients. We include general information about multicultural issues when offering such services to this population, social and cultural factors that can contribute to the success and effectiveness of a therapeutic relationship with Mexican American clients, and potential techniques, skills, and strategies that can be used to engage clients from this group. We also discuss the importance of creating awareness and sensitivity that can allow a practitioner to offer the most successful interventions possible. In the next chapter, we discuss tests and measurements when working with Mexican Americans.

Chapter 10

Psychological Assessments and Evaluations for Mexican Americans

Mental health professionals have to be culturally competent and sensitive in the many roles they play. The process of conducting psychological assessments and evaluations for Mexican Americans is no exception, and clinicians should be mindful of using the appropriate instruments. At a conference lecture that addressed multicultural issues, an audience member asked about the use of some psychological instruments to measure a person's intellectual level, or IQ. He asked the presenter about the tools that could evaluate a Mexican American client who only speaks Spanish. Another member of the audience, an experienced psychologist who did not speak Spanish, said there was a Spanish version of the Wechsler Adult Intelligence Scale (WAIS), so it would not be difficult to measure the Spanish-speaking Mexican American client's IQ. The WAIS is one of the most widely utilized IQ tests for adults because of its friendly instructions, its easy scoring process, and the general information it can provide about a person's general cognitive functioning. It would be ideal if this instrument could be used with all Spanish-speaking populations. The presenter, using caution and taking advantage of this opportunity to provide information about multicultural sensitivity, explained that even though the WAIS is in Spanish, the norms used when translating it were from Puerto Rico and, therefore, it would not be the best measure if used for other Spanish-speaking populations, such as Mexican American.

Conferences and lectures serve as a method to provide and acquire information about different topics. Because the psychologist who suggested the use of the WAIS spoke only English, he probably never used the instrument in Spanish. Engaging in this conversation during the conference allowed the presenter to clarify and provide new information that will surely be effective in the way he perceives instruments for Spanish-speaking populations. The question that came to my mind was, is it possible some Spanish-speaking or bilingual practitioners do not have this background information and may utilize psychological measures that would not provide the most accurate information about a Spanish-speaking client? If so, why does this occur?

I believe part of the problem is the lack of cultural sensitivity in the field in general (Purnell, 2013; Purnell and Pontious, 2014). As discussed in previous chapters, the understanding of cultural factors and being culturally competent can determine whether an intervention is appropriate and effective. The goal of this chapter is, rather than solely to provide a list of instruments that can be used for the Mexican American population, to create awareness and sensitivity when working with this population, ensuring that the instruments and approaches are not biased and can provide an accurate measure of whatever is being evaluated.

The other general caution I would like to provide is against the idea that such tools will provide magical information that will reveal a person's deepest secrets. One of the most important rules that we have to follow when working with psychological tools is that tools do not diagnose conditions. Clinicians who use such tools diagnose conditions. Any test result is not as meaningful as the analysis a clinician can provide. Utilizing measures and tools in counseling and psychological practice can be a great way to obtain more information about any topic. Unless the clinician has been trained in the administration, interpretation, and analysis of data that were obtained from the tools, however, the tools are useless.

FINDING APPROPRIATE TOOLS

As I was finishing this chapter, I was invited to lecture at a conference. I shared with the audience the challenges I have experienced finding the most appropriate set of tools or measures to accurately provide information about Mexican American clients and Spanish-speaking clients. Only a handful of the hundreds in attendance seemed to agree. That may be because there are not as many bilingual or Spanish-speaking clinicians in the field, but it may also be a reflection of this issue not being known due to a lack of understanding of cultural factors.

When selecting an instrument for Mexican Americans, it is important to ensure the instrument has adequate validity and reliability. Validity refers to the extent to which any instrument measures what it is intending to measure. Reliability refers to the consistency to which an instrument measures what it intends to measure (Anastasi and Urbina, 1997). Consider the following example: A person weighs himself every day to determine if he has lost weight after engaging in physical activity. If he used a scale that is valid and reliable, it will always provide him with his actual weight (validity), and if he weighs himself several times consecutively, he should see the same weight (reliability). Now, say this man is not happy with his weight and decides to modify the measure of weight by decreasing it 5 pounds. Instead of showing his actual weight, the scale would show he is 5 pounds lighter (not valid). However, if he were to weigh himself consecutively, he would obtain the same measure if the scale were reliable, although not valid.

The best way to determine if an instrument has appropriate validity and reliability is by looking at the studies conducted to create and develop the instrument. If it is a standardized instrument, it is necessary to know the areas and the characteristics of the population used to create and norm the instrument.

Standardization refers to "uniformity of procedure in administering and scoring the test" (Anastasi and Urbina, 1997). In other words, an instrument that has been standardized should be administered to every person in the same way, and the scoring is established and should follow the same rules for every examinee.

Another important related concept is norms, the average performance to which a person's performance or score is compared (Anastasi and Urbina, 1997). Imagine we were to create a standardized instrument that measured knowledge and use of Spanglish. Keeping in mind the concept of standardization, we know we would have to make sure the instrument is administered in the exact same way for every person being evaluated. But once a person was evaluated with this instrument, how would we determine if the score the person obtained reveals an extensive or deficient knowledge of Spanglish? One way to do this is through norms. Before using this instrument, we would need to establish what each score means. We can compare each person's performance with the average performance using this instrument, which we would obtain through research studies and as part of the development of the instrument. Norm comes from normal, or average, so the performance obtained would be compared to the average of many people's performances (Anastasi and Urbina, 1997). To develop norms, we would have to utilize the instruments in research studies and obtain the average of scores of the participants. We could then determine an average performance and whether a person's performance on this imaginative test would reflect a deficient or extensive knowledge of Spanglish.

Why would we spend time talking about this if this book is not intended to focus on research or psychological tools only? When working with Mexican Americans, it is imperative that a clinician using psychological instruments is aware of norms and standardization as well as the characteristics of the group that participated in the development of such instruments. It is then possible to determine whether the instruments are appropriate for the Mexican American population.

Also, just because an instrument is effective and has been shown to be a good measurement for a domain or a variable does not mean it would be effective for every population, including Mexican Americans. Consider the WAIS, for example. This instrument is one of the most commonly used cognitive measures. Were Mexican Americans used in the development of its norms? Yes. Were they English-speaking? Yes. Can this instrument be used to evaluate Spanish-speaking Mexican Americans to measure intellectual level? No, because the norms were obtained by administering the instrument in English, not Spanish. Even if this instrument was translated into Spanish, it would have to be normed to the Mexican American population to be accurate and useful.

If we were to translate the instrument and administer it to Spanish-speaking Mexican Americans without adjusting the norms to fit the characteristics of the population, the results would not necessarily reveal accurate information. Due to cultural differences and specific characteristics of the population, comparing it with another population may result in a score that is not accurately measuring what is intended. For example, imagine I was assessing intelligence and asked people to define *barbacoa*. This is a typical food in Mexican American communities, and it may be different depending on where it is consumed. If a person has not been exposed to the Mexican American population or this food, he or she is unlikely to answer correctly. However, this incorrect response would not necessarily be a reflection of his or her intellectual functioning. We will talk more about intellectual/cognitive measures later in this chapter.

TYPES OF INSTRUMENTS

A wide variety of instruments can be used when working with Mexican Americans. However, it is important to consider the individual characteristics of each client to ensure the instrument will serve the intended purpose.

Structured versus Unstructured Interviews

As we discussed in Chapter 8, unstructured interviews are those that do not follow a uniform pattern, can change and be modified throughout the interview, and do not have to be performed in a specific, established manner. Structured interviews are established and require a certain structure to be followed without deviation. These can be used if the client requires a very clear structure to be able to provide the necessary information, such as people who display tangential or circumstantial thinking, jumping from one topic to the next, or providing extensive but unnecessary details.

In the Mexican American population, the use of these instruments varies depending on the individual's characteristics. Generally, however, the cultural norms and features indicate a large number of Mexican Americans would probably prefer and benefit from unstructured interviews rather than having to follow a structured interview (Bernard, 2006).

Standardized Mental Status Measure

In addition to administering a person's mental state using a nonstandardized approach, which was described in detail in Chapter 8, some tools are designed to assess mental status functioning in a more standardized manner. For these instruments to be effective, it is important to first consider that language is crucial, and if a client is Spanish-speaking, then the instrument must be in Spanish. The clinician must be cautious and have a thorough and deep understanding of the language factors and differences among regions and contexts. For example, a Mexican American raised in Mexico City who arrived in the United States two years ago is likely to perform differently on some tools that use information based on U.S. society than a Mexican American born in the northern states of Mexico next to the U.S. border who has been in the United States for 20 years. This does not mean the instrument would not be useful at all for the client from Mexico City, but the clinician has to be cautious about how to use the data obtained.

Three of the most common standardized instruments used to measure mental status are the Mini Mental Status Exam (MMSE), the Saint Louis University Mental Status (SLUMS) Exam, and the Montreal Cognitive Assessment (MoCA). These instruments are usually used to detect a cognitive disorder, but they can also be used to assess cognitive functioning and factors that can influence it.

The MMSE was originally developed in 1975 by Marshall and Susan Folstein to assist in evaluating general cognitive impairment. Several variations of this instrument have been made, and it continues to be one of the most commonly utilized to assess severe cognitive dysfunction (Buckingham, Mackor, Miller, Pullman, Molloy, Grisby, et al., 2013; Ismail, Rajji, and Shulman, 2010). It is formed by 11 different questions that fall into two separate sections. The first assesses if the person is oriented, if there are deficits or problems with attention levels, and if there are issues with memory processes. The second evaluates language skills through verbal and written tasks, as well as visual-spatial processes. The individual's performance is then given a score up to 30, which suggests there is no cognitive dysfunction and the individual functions at a normal level (Buckingham et al., 2013). This instrument has a Spanish version. However, a main limitation of the MMSE is that minority groups, particularly the Mexican American population, tend to score lower than European Americans, suggesting it does not moderate for cultural factors (Martínez-Ramírez, Rodríguez-Violante, González-Latapi, Cervantes-Arriaga, Camacho-Ordoñez, Morales-Briceño, et al., 2014).

The SLUMS Exam was developed to assess a person's capacity in the areas of orientation, attention, and concentration and memory, and areas pertaining to executive functioning (Buckingham et al., 2013). This instrument, just like the MMSE, uses a maximum score of 30 and measures impairment based on incorrect items. In other words, the lower the score a person obtains, the more cognitive impairment the person may experience. The different subtests on the SLUMS exam assess in more detail cognitive functioning when compared with the MMSE (Buckingham et al., 2013). Furthermore, the SLUMS exam has been more effective in detecting Mild Neurocognitive Impairment than the MMSE (Tariq, Tumosa, Chibnall, Perry, and Morley, 2006). People who suffered from mild neurocognitive disorder obtained a high score on the MMSE. For an individual to obtain a low score on the MMSE, there must be significant cognitive impairment (Tariq et al., 2006). This instrument also has a Spanish version, which can be very effective in measuring dysfunction.

Just like the SLUMS exam, the MoCA has been shown to be more effective than the MMSE to detect a mild neurocognitive disorder. The maximum score with this instrument is also 30, and a score ranging from 26 to 30 falls within a normal level of functioning. Similarly, it assesses cognitive areas of attention and concentration, language abilities, memory through verbal means, areas related to the executive functioning of an individual, and visual-spatial abilities. This instrument recently went through a process of normalization, and the results revealed that it is sensitive to level of education. For example, people with a higher level of education tended to score higher than people with a lower level. Results also showed it is sensitive to age, but not as much. In other words, the change of performance due to age was not overtly different. The median of scores seemed to differ more with age on the group with a lower level of education. For example, people from ages 30 to 40 scored almost 3 points higher than those from ages 50 to 60. However, this difference was less than 2 points in people with a higher level of education (Rossetti, Lacritz, Cullum, and Weiner, 2011). Because of this, caution is encouraged when using this instrument for the

Mexican American population, as this group has a lower rate of college education than other cultural groups (Ennis, Rios-Vargas, and Albert, 2011).

One of the most important limitations of these instruments is that they do not account for any external factors which could influence or impair the individual's cognitive functioning. For example, one of the symptoms of a major depressive disorder is difficulty concentrating. A person with severe depression may experience cognitive difficulties that, without knowing the affective component of the person's state at the time of the evaluation, could mislead clinicians to believe the individual may suffer from a cognitive disorder. This observation brings us back to the earlier point that psychological measures and instruments do not diagnose mental health conditions. They only offer information, and it is up to the clinician to determine what that information means.

COGNITIVE MEASURES

One of the most difficult tasks for a clinician is to select culturally and linguistically appropriate instruments for some minority groups. This does not have to be the case for Mexican Americans, particularly if they are second or third generation and speak English, as most of the instruments normed in the United States are in English. Nevertheless, if the Mexican American client does not speak English or arrived in the United States recently, finding an adequate and reliable instrument may be a challenge.

Cognitive Evaluations

When we refer to IQ, we need to consider a variety of mental abilities (Anastasi and Urbina, 1997). A single mental ability would not be the only measure that would give information about intelligence; thus, instruments that measure intelligence level need to include a variety of tasks, some verbal and some nonverbal. Some address and evaluate visual-spatial abilities and others general information about the use of language. Memory is usually an area IQ tests measure as part of general intelligence. However, these subtests can also provide information about how much data a person's mind can retain and whether general neurocognitive dysfunction exists. Having a normed and standardized tool that can measure all of these abilities and that is appropriate for the population with which a clinician is working can provide a lot of information for treatment plan development. Unfortunately, having such a tool is not always the case. Particularly with clients who do not speak English, it is difficult to near impossible to find a single tool or set of instruments that can provide as much information about a person's mental abilities and functioning.

Remember the example shared about the WAIS in Spanish, but normed in people from Puerto Rico. At that point, language may not be the issue, but culture may affect the scores. Consider a study published in 2011 attempting to compare the adaptation of a normed instrument in different populations. Just as with the Wechsler Adult Intelligence Scale being one of the most commonly used tools to measure intelligence in adults, Wechsler's Intelligence Scale for Children does the same with children. This instrument is in its fourth edition and, like the WAIS, it is composed of several subtests that ultimately derive to a full-scale IQ score. This instrument was originally developed in English, but due to the needs of different locations, several versions focus on different populations. In the United States, a Hispanic version was standardized with 851 children of Hispanic descent from Puerto Rico, Cuba, South America, and Central America who resided in the United States. This adaptation has instructions in English, but responses in Spanish are appropriate, so the evaluator must be bilingual. Furthermore, a WISC-IV version exists in Mexico, completely in Spanish and normed with children from different parts of the country. When comparing the versions of the WISC-IV by administering it to children from the population it intended to evaluate, the results were different. In other words, even though children from different backgrounds and using their corresponding version of the WISC-IV obtained the same raw score in some subtests, these were converted into different standard scores. However, these scores were not as significantly different as if the children had been evaluated with a version of the WISC-IV that had not been standardized or normed with their population (Sánchez-Escobedo, Hollingworth, and Fina, 2011).

Achievement Tests

In addition to obtaining measures of general intellectual functioning, psychological instruments measure a person's ability to learn academic information. These are called achievement tests or aptitude tests, and, although several exist in the United States in English, some have been designed to measure academic ability in Spanish. Aptitude tests must also be normed and standardized. The same problems as with IQ tests may emerge, as these instruments may be influenced by cultural factors. The question that clinicians should keep in mind is, if a Mexican American examinee attended school in Mexico, can any of these tools reveal an accurate measure? It is possible that, just as with the case of families in border towns, students attended school in Mexico and now attend school in the United States, which may be an indication that the administration of such an instrument could be appropriate. Keep in mind, however, the importance of the level of acculturation in deciding which instrument to utilize and afterward what the data reveal about the client and his or her abilities.

The most widely used achievement test for Mexican Americans who speak only Spanish is the Batería III Woodcock-Muñoz. This test was adapted from the Woodcock-Johnson Tests of Cognitive Abilities and is particularly useful because it contains both achievement and IQ measures. It is in Spanish and has been normed to a Spanish-speaking population in the United States (Ardonio, n.d.).

FORENSIC EVALUATIONS OF MEXICAN AMERICANS

Usually the term *forensic evaluation* can include a variety of procedures related to a legal setting. For example, a forensic evaluation can be conducted during a divorce to determine the best setting for the child. It can also help establish whether a person committed a crime due to symptoms of a mental illness. This section includes a general description of forensic evaluations commonly used in psychology and offers some considerations when conducting them on someone from a Mexican American background.

Overview of Forensic Evaluations

Before conducting any type of evaluation, the clinician or evaluator needs to determine its purpose. Knowing the referral question will determine what needs to happen for the question to be answered. When the referral question is related to the legal system, it can be answered conducting a forensic evaluation. Some instruments and procedures used during other types of evaluations can also be used in forensic evaluations, but the answer to the question must always be kept in mind.

CUSTODY EVALUATIONS

It is common in a custody dispute to consult with a psychologist to determine where the child or children would be better off. The purpose of these evaluations is to provide information about the potential placements, always maintaining the best interest of the child as a priority. One problem with this concept is that the best interest of the child is broad and can mean many things to many people (Emery, Otto, and O'Donohue, 2005). Furthermore, evidence suggests that the system is in some ways flawed and needs a lot of reform in order to be more effective not only for children, but also for parents fighting for custody (Emery *et al.*, 2005). Three main recommendations have been proposed to assist with the custody process. First, it is important to assist individuals in resolving their conflicts not in the courtroom but through mediation and other means. This action is likely to promote better relationships and give the child a better environment rather than one where the parents are constantly fighting or where the child doesn't have a parent at all. Another recommendation is a revision of the law that makes the concept "best interest of the child" more specific, with clear guidelines that can be easily identified. Lastly, practitioners and evaluators should make recommendations based only on the data obtained from the evaluation. The data have to be scientifically based and must not include emotions or assumptions from the evaluator (Emery *et al.*, 2005).

The divorce rate for Mexican Americans may not be as high as other ethnic or cultural groups (Padilla and Borrero, 2006), but Mexican Americans still go through divorce. Several factors may complicate custody evaluations, such as undocumented status. It is not always the case that an undocumented parent will not receive custody; other social and legal obstacles need to be addressed to ultimately offer the best setting for the child.

CAPACITY AND COMPETENCY EVALUATIONS

In some situations, evaluators may be asked to conduct capacity evaluations. These may require only a clinical interview and a brief Mental Status Exam (which we discuss in Chapter 8), but other tools may be needed to answer referral questions. They also may require collateral information to ensure that the most accurate picture is obtained.

It is important to clarify the differences between capacity and competency evaluations. Capacity refers to the person's ability to make "rational decisions" (Leo, 1999). These evaluations can provide information about the client's psychological abilities and whether the client is able to "understand, appreciate, and manipulate information and form rational decisions" (Leo, 1999). This decision process is particularly relevant to medical decisions. For example, does the person have the psychological ability to make decisions that are beneficial for him or her? Capacity is a medical concept and, as opposed to competency, is not a legal term. Competency is an individual's ability to participate in an activity (Leo, 1999). This definition is very broad, but it is usually defined as such because it can be applied to several different settings. For example, a concept commonly used in forensic settings is competency to stand trial. The judicial system is designed to assure there is justice. When a person commits a crime and is arrested, he or she is entitled to a fair trial, with the opportunity to present his or her side of the story. For the process to be considered just, the person accused must be able to defend himself or herself and participate in the court system. Whenever the person is not able to participate, particularly due to mental illness, the person may be declared incompetent to stand trial, meaning he or she is unable to fulfill certain areas that determine the ability to participate. Every state may have different measures of competency. They usually include the following expectations, though there may be more, depending on the state (Melton, Petrila, Poythress, Slobogin, Lyons Jr., and Otto, 2007):

1. Being able to comprehend his or her own legal situation.
2. Being able to comprehend the charges (i.e., what they mean and how they came to exist).
3. Having a general understanding of the possible pleas.
4. Being able to comprehend the potential consequences of the charges.
5. Being capable of understanding the role of the attorneys (defense and prosecutor) and the judge in the courtroom.
6. Showing the ability to communicate clearly and effectively with the attorney.
7. Providing information that can assist in collecting evidence and identifying witnesses.
8. Assisting the attorney with the defense by helping develop strategies to win the case.
9. Demonstrating appropriate courtroom behavior.
10. Making good decisions pertaining to the strategy to follow during the trial.

The severity of impairment must be substantial for a person to be determined by the court to be incompetent to stand trial, and mental illness alone does not guarantee a person is incompetent. In most states, a licensed psychologist or physician can conduct competency evaluations, but they must be ordered by the court.

Mexican Americans do not make up the highest number of prisoners in jail systems, according to the 2010 U.S. Census, but they may need to be evaluated for competency to stand trial. As with other evaluations, it is important for the clinician to be culturally sensitive, and if the person speaks only Spanish, it would be preferable that the clinician also speaks Spanish. Particularly because a large number of patients found incompetent to stand trial suffer from symptoms of psychosis, it is important to distinguish what may be part of a psychotic process and not part of a cultural practice (e.g., a folk healer who reports travels to other realms to battle demons).

SOME LIMITATIONS ABOUT FORENSIC EVALUATIONS

As with other types of evaluations, forensic evaluations are not perfect. Several of the referral questions have to do with predicting future behavior. Although it is possible to identify risk factors of a potential likelihood that events may happen (e.g., which parent could provide the best environment for a child), it is not possible to predict accurately all the time. Additionally, some referral questions may be difficult to answer and are asked from a legal perspective rather than from a clinical perspective, which can complicate the evaluation process.

SUMMARY

In this chapter, we look at psychological evaluations and the factors that can contribute to their effectiveness with Mexican American clients. We discuss issues related to multicultural competency and sensitivity and different types of instruments for conducting psychological evaluations for the Mexican American population. The content of this chapter is supplemental to the information presented previously, but a very large and extensive body of knowledge was not presented but is still essential to understand. The main goal of this chapter is to encourage people to be more mindful when selecting instruments and to be sensitive when the data are being analyzed and interpreted rather than assuming such factors are not necessary in psychology and in conducting psychological evaluations. In the next chapter, we discuss crisis management.

Chapter 11

Crisis Interventions

Several years ago, I worked with clients on an outpatient basis who suffered from severe mental illness, conducting crisis screenings to determine whether they were in need of inpatient psychiatric treatment. To meet hospitalization criteria, clients had to demonstrate that they were in immediate danger to themselves, were a danger to others, or were impaired to the point of endangering themselves, such as with schizophrenia (e.g., wandering into the middle of the road without being aware of it). On one occasion, I had a call from an emergency room informing me that one of my clients, a 55-year-old Hispanic Mexican American woman who suffered from schizoaffective disorder, had arrived via ambulance after expressing that she was a danger to herself. I met with her at the ER where she was eating a sandwich while lying in bed. Her affect seemed bright, and she seemed to be in no distress. As I conducted the crisis screening, I found no evidence she was actively suicidal, homicidal, in imminent danger to herself or others, or that her symptoms of psychosis were causing her to be significantly impaired. She reported only that she was feeling somewhat sad because her sister and mother, whom she had lived with since she began having symptoms of psychosis at around age 26, had left for California to visit some family members. At the end of my assessment, I explained to her that she did not appear to meet criteria for inpatient treatment and I recommended she return home. She said she was feeling lonely and sad and did not want to be alone. She added that at the local psychiatric hospital, where she had been numerous times for treatment, she knew there would be other patients and staff with her 24 hours a day. I reiterated that based on her responses to the assessment, she did not meet criteria for inpatient treatment. She then asked, "What do I have to say so you can send me to the hospital?"

The purpose of sharing this story is to explain that not all crisis screenings, assessments, or evaluations may result in inpatient treatment or law enforcement involvement. It is important to thoroughly evaluate the client and determine the level of risk in order to make a recommendation. The second point I would like to share is that, whatever we know as a crisis in mental health (i.e., danger to self, danger to others, or danger of deterioration or impairment caused by severe symptoms) may not be consistent with what some people may consider a crisis. In the example I shared, the client's situation in which her mother and sister were away in California was a crisis to her. It is important to consider family involvement in mental health treatment and crisis management, particularly with Mexican American clients. This consideration is essential to the mental and emotional stability of Mexican Americans with mental illness.

Some of the jobs I have had in the mental health setting have dealt with crisis interventions. I work in a region where there is a predominant number of Mexican Americans, and several interventions and cultural characteristics may be viewed as normal in this part of the country. Many other areas in the United States are more diverse, and this information may not be the norm. That makes the information presented in this chapter important when handling crises experienced by Mexican American clients. The chapter includes information about crises and a definition of "crisis" and how to assess it. It also includes factors that can contribute to an exacerbation of situations which can eventually become a crisis. Lastly, it contains information about culturally appropriate interventions based on Mexican American cultural characteristics.

WHAT IS A CRISIS?

If we asked 100 people their definition of a crisis, we may get 100 different definitions. Before we can talk about assessment and interventions, we need to first understand what they mean, particularly in mental health and in Mexican American populations. According to the Merriam-Webster online dictionary, a crisis is "a difficult or dangerous situation that needs serious attention" (Merriam-Webster.com). This definition is very general, and many interpretations can define instances of crisis. For example, the woman from the scenario at the beginning of the chapter viewed her mother and sister going to California and leaving her by herself as a crisis. While other people would view that situation as ordinary or not dangerous or difficult, some people may consider it hard to contend with.

I remember attending a training session where the presenter defined a crisis in mental health as a situation in which a person has lost control and that has the potential to lead to danger. As mentioned, a crisis in a mental health setting strictly refers to the level of danger a person may have to self or to others, either through self-intent or through circumstances that would keep him or her or others from safety.

DEFINING DANGER TO SELF

In mental health, danger to self can refer to many things. For example, if a person punches herself when angry or bangs her head into a wall, she can be in danger of causing significant damage to self. This scenario differs from a person who cuts his arm superficially when feeling very sad, not with the intent of killing himself, but in an attempt to substitute emotional pain with physical pain. Another type of danger to self can result from severe symptoms that impair cognitive functioning and judgment, such as when a person suffers from dementia or a psychotic disorder. If the person is not able to function adequately enough to live independently and she has no support, she may be in danger that can eventually become imminent. Consider symptoms of psychosis and how they can exacerbate this state of mind. If a person experiences auditory hallucinations in the form of voices that tell him the only way to save humanity is by jumping off the 12th floor of a hotel, and that he will be given wings as he does this so he does not harm himself, he may be at risk of engaging in something likely to cause death, even though he did not have the active intention of harming himself.

Another type of danger to self results from having suicidal ideation or from attempting suicide. Suicide refers to intentionally ending one's own life. Crisis management obviously does not occur after a successful suicide attempt; the interventions occur to prevent any danger to self, including suicidality. Although it may seem simple to define suicidality as part of danger to self, several factors need to be considered when assessing risk. We present some information about suicidal assessment later in this chapter.

DEFINING DANGER TO OTHERS

The first thought many people have when they hear the concept of danger to others is homicidality, or intentionally ending someone else's life. However, the concept can involve other scenarios. For example, if a person has poor impulse control and difficulty managing her own anger, she may explode and attack others without the immediate intention of killing anyone, but with the intention of hurting them physically in order to release her anger. I have assessed different clients with similar characteristics as the ones described here, and a common area among them is that, whenever they are exposed to situations that elicit intense anger, they do not think much and just act before realizing what they are doing. They may not have a premeditated desire to end a person's life, but they may still hurt others. Additionally, as with danger to self, a person can experience symptoms that can impair judgment or cognitive functioning. Consider the following example: A 45-year-old Mexican American male who suffers from schizophrenia and delusional thinking that consists of believing people at a convenience store are plotting to kill him and the only way out of the situation is to attack them first may be at risk of causing harm to others. Another example is a person who is in a state of mind where she cannot function independently, is not aware of where she is or who she is, and who does something that can endanger others, even without intent, such as driving a car while being in such a state of mind.

WHAT TO DO IN CRISES?

Before discussing the ethical and legal actions needed if a clinician is faced with a crisis, we need to explain a few things. Among many ethical and professional expectations in clinical professions such as psychology, counseling, or social work, one of the most important has to do with confidentiality rules (Fisher, 2003). The reason for this is that, in a clinical setting, a person is likely to reveal very personal information he or she would not necessarily want known. This information may include thoughts of danger to self or others. By law and as part of the ethical standards of practice, clinicians must present clients with a notice of privacy practices, which must include information about limits of confidentiality (Fisher, 2003). Basically, a client must be informed that, even though it is imperative confidentiality is maintained in a therapeutic relationship, information pertaining to danger to self or others may be disclosed to the appropriate parties without written consent from the client.

This was not always the case, and a specific case changed the way we process such information. In the late 1960s, a citizen of India, Prosenjit Poddar, was studying naval architecture at the University of California, Berkeley. He became romantically interested in Tatiana Tarasoff. When she said she was not interested in a long-term romantic relationship with him, Poddar became distressed and sought psychotherapy at the university's student health services center. His psychotherapist thought Poddar had become obsessed with Tarasoff to the point of wanting to purchase a gun. After several sessions and with concerns regarding Poddar's emotional stability, the therapist consulted with his supervisor, who recommended contacting the campus police regarding the potential of Tarasoff getting hurt. Law enforcement officials interviewed Poddar and found him rational and not a danger to Tarasoff. After the encounter with the police, Poddar never returned to the clinic, and about two months later, in 1969, he stabbed Tarasoff to death. Tarasoff's family sued the university regents and all the clinical staff involved in the case. The tragedy resulted in several changes to clinical and legal rules. Mental health practice changed in several states, and it became mandatory for clinicians to warn third parties if evidence existed to suggest their client had the potential of hurting them (Koocher and Keith-Spiegel, 1998).

Since the ruling in the Tarasoff case, clinicians who practice in states where the ruling was adopted must notify individuals whom clients may harm. Texas, where I practice, is one of the states that did not adopt this rule. However, clinicians must notify law enforcement and do everything in their capacity and within reason to reduce the possibility of anyone getting hurt. Contacting law enforcement is one option. Mental health commitments obtained through judges also permit peace officers to detain and transport clients who may be in danger to self or others to an inpatient psychiatric facility (Koocher and Keith-Spiegel, 1998).

Here is a brief synopsis of the general steps to take in a situation in which a person may be an imminent danger to self or others: Anyone with a clinical license to practice in any state, or clinicians who work in settings where it is not required to have a license, such as a community clinic where the clinician is in charge only of obtaining psychosocial history, must be aware of state laws, regulations, and standards of practice that describe the process to follow whenever a person is a danger to self or others. As soon as clinicians determine there is imminent danger to self or others, they are usually required to contact law enforcement. If the Tarasoff Rule has been adopted in the state where the clinician practices, the clinician may have to contact the person who may be in danger (Koocher and Keith-Spiegel, 1998).

ASSESSMENT OF CRISES

In Chapters 8 and 10, we presented information about conducting clinical interviews and evaluations in different settings, such as forensic evaluations to determine the best setting for a child going through a custody dispute. When conducting screenings, assessments, or evaluations to determine the risk of danger in a crisis, and to determine what would be the most appropriate and effective intervention, several elements are the same as those present in other evaluations or assessments. For example, conducting a Mental Status Exam for diagnostic clarification is essential to determine if a person suffers from Major Depressive Disorder or Bipolar Disorder. It is also necessary when conducting an assessment to explore the risk and the nature and severity of a crisis. There are specific elements to look for when exploring risk in a crisis situation.

ASSESSING DANGER TO SELF

Because danger to self can present in different ways, it is important to have a thorough understanding of the situation before making recommendations. As previously stated, a person who bangs his head into a wall when angry or frustrated may not require inpatient treatment. This level of care is appropriate for people in imminent danger to self or others and would be more adequate for someone with active suicidal ideation or someone who attempted suicide.

SUICIDE RISK FACTORS

As discussed in Chapter 10, assessments and evaluations are available to help answer questions about a person's personality and behavior, including what can be expected in the future for an individual, but it is important to understand their limitations and the fact that it may not be possible to completely predict what will happen. Nevertheless, some factors can be considered to determine the level of risk and potential interventions. The Tool for Assessment of Suicide Risk, modified version (TASRm), is an instrument developed to assist clinicians to identify important risk suicide factors (Chehil and Kutcher, 2012). As mentioned in Chapter 10, psychological tools do not diagnose individuals but provide information for the clinician to make decisions and determine the level of risk. This tool divides suicide risk factors into three major categories: Individual Risk Profile, Symptom Risk Profile, and Interview Risk Profile (Chehil and Kutcher, 2012).

The Individual Risk Profile contains primarily demographic information found to be associated with suicidal behavior. For example, if an individual is in the age range of 13–35, or is 65 years or older, he or she may be at a higher risk. Additionally, males are more likely to commit suicide. Family history is another important factor. The presence of suicidal behavior in family members or a history of mental illness can indicate a higher risk for suicide. The client's own psychiatric diagnosis may also increase the likelihood of suicide, as will chronic and debilitating medical illness, poor social support, substance abuse, family conflict, violence, poor coping mechanisms for stress, a history of physical, verbal, or emotional abuse, and a history of suicide attempts or self-harm (Chehil and Kutcher, 2012).

Symptom Risk Profile presents information about the following psychiatric symptoms correlated with suicidal behavior: depression or dysphoria, severe anhedonia, intense emotional response related to anxiety, hopelessness, shame or feelings of humiliation, guilt, loneliness or isolation, anger, withdrawal, feelings of worthlessness, poor judgment or affected reasoning to make appropriate decisions, poor emotional regulation, impulsivity, aggression, excessive and troublesome substance abuse, and psychosis in the form of commanding hallucinations (Chehil and Kutcher, 2012).

In the Interview Profile, you may also identify factors that can be discovered during the Mental Status Exam. It explores areas specifically related to suicidal behavior, such as current suicidal ideation, current intent to commit suicide, a history of suicide attempts, access to lethal methods to commit suicide, recent substance use, triggers such as a recent loss or significant psychosocial stressors or problems that may appear unresolvable, intolerable emotional response, and command auditory hallucinations (Chehil and Kutcher, 2012).

ASSESSING DANGER TOWARD OTHERS

Several demographic characteristics have been directly associated with aggressive behavior or violence. Many people may have the potential of being aggressive, but some factors can increase the likelihood of violence and aggression. Research has shown that males are more likely to be aggressive and violent compared with women (Zeichner, Parrott, and Frey, 2003; Archer, 2004). The late teens and early twenties have been correlated to aggressive behavior (Archer, 2004). Individuals with lower IQ scores tend to be more violent (Huesmann, Eron, and Yarmel, 1987). And people from low socioeconomic status have been associated with aggressive behavior (Farrington, 1989). Several research studies have associated drug and alcohol abuse or dependence with aggressive behavior (Hoff, Hallisey, and Hoff, 2009). In fact, other pathologies such as schizophrenia may be perceived by the general population as a significant factor increasing aggressive behavior and violence, but drug and alcohol disorders are greater predictors of violence (Hoff *et al.*, 2009).

AFFECTIVE VERSUS PREDATORY VIOLENCE

Some authors have classified violence into two major categories: affective and predatory. Affective violence is usually a result of a perceived threat, when the attacker feels trapped or threatened, and the person may feel there is no alternative than to fight. Predatory violence is usually planned, premeditated, and emotionally detached. The best example is seen in people suffering from Antisocial Personality Disorder (American Psychiatric Association, 2013).

HOMICIDE RISK FACTORS

There are also different ways to assess homicidality. The Assault & Homicidal Danger Assessment Tool (Hoff et al., 2009) classifies the risk of danger into five categories. The first is "No predictable risk of assault or homicide," which is assigned when there is no history of aggressive behavior or homicidal ideation and where there may be occasional alcohol consumption and a generally satisfied support system.

The second level, "Low risk of assault or homicide," is assigned when infrequent episodes of aggression and homicidal ideation occur, but no problems with impulsivity exist or a history of homicidal attempts; occasional alcohol consumption and episodes of anger and verbal aggression can be present. In this level, there is still a generally satisfied support system.

The third level is classified as "Moderate risk of assault or homicide" and is characterized by regular homicidal ideation and urges to kill others, but with no clear or concrete plan to do so. The individual in this category has experienced problems with impulsivity and periods of verbal aggression while under the influence of alcohol or drugs. There are also constant arguments between the person and his or her significant other.

The fourth level, "High risk of homicide," consists of a plan to commit homicide and reachable methods to achieve it. A noted history of substance use is also present as well as regular episodes of acting out in front of others, but with no homicide attempt. There are constant verbal aggressions toward family and significant others and some periods of physical assaults toward others.

The highest level of risk is called "Very high risk of homicide" and is characterized by a current high-lethal plan to commit homicide, reachable methods, previous homicide attempts, impulse control problems, the need to try to "get even" with the person's significant other, and the risk of suicide (Hoff et al., 2009).

CRISIS INTERVENTIONS

When a crisis is identified, several steps must be taken to assist. It may be necessary for law enforcement to be involved; however, people going through a crisis may be receptive to help from their family and support system.

CRISIS PHONE LINE

One of the services available in most communities is a crisis phone line. This service can be part of a local mental health authority or clinic and provides support to those experiencing difficulties or in crisis. This service is usually available 24 hours a day, every day, and offers guidance, even directing the person to the most appropriate treatment. In some instances, the client de-escalates and feels relieved after speaking with a representative. However, the client may not de-escalate, and the professional may send emergency services, such as law enforcement, an ambulance, or a clinician who can determine whether the client needs inpatient psychiatric treatment (National Alliance on Mental Illness, 2010). If the person doesn't know a crisis phone line number, 911 can be used to seek out help in a crisis. Services are available in Spanish through the National Suicide Prevention Lifeline and other local resources for Mexican Americans who only speak Spanish (www.suicidepreventionlifeline.org).

MANAGEMENT OF CRISES

Several different models describe a series of steps to follow in a mental health crisis. Roberts and Ottens (2005) proposed a model for crisis intervention consisting of seven stages for assessing the situation and determining the best treatment setting and option for clients:

1. Prepare and perform a general assessment that includes a biopsychosocial perspective and explores the level of danger to self, including the intent to commit suicide, the means the person is considering, and how likely it is to occur (i.e., whether the person has a plan and is convinced he or she will succeed).
2. Explore and establish good rapport and a positive, collaborative therapeutic relationship.
3. Determine the precipitating events or stressors that led to the exacerbation of the crisis. Explore the current problems affecting the person immediately before and during the crisis.
4. Assist the client in exploring his or her feelings and emotions about the situation. For example, a person with suicidal ideation may be extremely angry in addition to feeling sad or hopeless.
5. Provide assistance exploring alternate coping mechanisms to address the symptoms that led to the crisis.
6. With the involvement of the client, formulate a plan of action that would assist the resolution of the crisis and permit the client to achieve the same level of functioning as before the crisis.
7. Prepare a session to follow up with the resolution of the crisis that will reinforce support.

HOSPITALIZATION, PARTIAL HOSPITALIZATION, AND RESPITE UNITS

It is not uncommon for people in crisis to go to an emergency room for help. The emergency room staff often will make arrangements for the client to be evaluated so that the most appropriate treatment can be offered. Psychiatric hospitalization may be inevitable, and a person in crisis may have to be hospitalized either on a voluntary basis or through a court commitment, but this is not the only type of outcome that may occur. In some cases, the crisis may subside with immediate support, and the person may just need to be monitored in a less-restrictive environment than a hospital, but with supervision and observation (U.S. Department of Health and Human Services. Substance Abuse and Mental Health Services Administration, Center for Mental Health Services, 2009).

The purpose of treatment is for the crisis to subside and for the person to regain prior functioning. It is important for clinicians to make follow-up referrals so that there can be a continuation of services after discharge (U.S. Department of Health and Human Services. Substance Abuse and Mental Health Services Administration, Center for Mental Health Services, 2009).

At a psychiatric hospital, clients in crisis are assessed usually by a psychiatrist, and it is determined whether the client needs inpatient treatment. In some cases, the physician may determine the client does not meet criteria for inpatient psychiatric treatment (e.g., if the crisis was caused by the use of a substance that has cleared). Clients who arrive at a psychiatric hospital, however, usually receive services, particularly if they arrive involuntarily.

ROLE OF LAW ENFORCEMENT IN CRISIS INTERVENTIONS

Every U.S. state has different laws and regulations to handle crises, but there are usually similar elements that address basic requirements. Some psychiatric hospitals are funded by the state; others are private, for-profit facilities that charge patients a fee. There may be voluntary and involuntary ways to be admitted to some of these hospitals, while others require people to be admitted only involuntarily, although their admission may change once they meet with a psychiatrist, collaboratively develop a treatment plan, and agree to receive treatment there.

In Texas, two types of mental health commitment exist. One can be created by law enforcement officials and originates if an officer thinks a person is experiencing mental health problems that may make him or her unsafe. For example, if an officer sees a person causing harm to self, he may enforce his legal power to commit the person for an evaluation and potential treatment.

The other type of treatment can be created by a judge. If a family member or friend thinks a sufficient danger or concern to commit someone exists, the person may explain the concerning symptoms and behaviors to a judge. If the judge thinks the client needs a mental health evaluation, the judge can sign a warrant to legally commit the person. A judge may also extend the commitment or even discharge the patient if he or she thinks the crisis has subsided and there is no imminent danger. (Stettin, Geller, Ragosta, Cohen, and Ghowrwal, 2014).

MENTAL HEALTH CRISES AND MEXICAN AMERICANS

When a Mexican American has a mental health crisis, the options, resources, and interventions available may be the same. However, culturally specific considerations need to be maintained when offering such services. For example, because of the collectivistic nature of the Mexican American culture, it may be more productive to offer crisis management and interventions involving family and others with whom the person feels comfortable (Sue and Sue, 2012). Language also is a very important part of the treatment and intervention. As discussed in previous chapters, being linguistically competent can increase the effectiveness of the treatment and the appropriate assessment. A few years ago, I assessed a 45-year-old Spanish-speaking Mexican American at a psychiatric hospital for treatment of severe depression and auditory hallucinations. She had lost her husband three months before and said she could hear her husband's voice. The client was prescribed an antipsychotic medication in addition to an antidepressant. Keep in mind that in the Mexican American population, it is not uncommon for some to perceive the voice of people they have lost or to experience other unusual perceptions that may not be a sign of psychopathology. After discussing in detail the nature of the hallucinations, she revealed that she only heard her husband's voice in her home, while asleep, and that she never heard the voice while awake. Part of the issue here is not cultural, but clinical. Hallucinations experienced solely while asleep are not symptoms of psychosis, but rather could be part of a dream. The patient reported that when she lost her mother she experienced the same situation in which she could hear her voice, while asleep, and that it eventually went away.

Sometimes crisis may be perceived by society as a sign of weakness or significant impairment. Males may be less inclined to accept that they have problems, while women may be more willing to accept that they are going through a crisis (Englander, Yáñez, and Barney, 2012). It may also be difficult for Mexican Americans to accept Western medicine approaches to mental health, and they may feel comfortable addressing crises with folk medical healers or family members who can provide comfort and support.

Spirituality has been identified as a protective factor for mental illness and can be used to manage crises. Because a characteristic of Mexican American groups is following religions and being affiliated with churches (López, 2015), it is important to explore whether religion can help the individual going through a crisis. If so, incorporate this as part of the recovery process.

Finally, in the Mexican American population, it is important to consider the disparity of power and authority in a clinical relationship. Clients are more likely to perceive their clinicians as authorities who know better, and that can significantly influence their recovery. Because of this, while establishing rapport, the clients may feel more comfortable knowing the clinician is an expert in the area and can help them. This trust would instill a sense of hope in their situation and may assist in resolving the crisis.

SUMMARY

In this chapter, I present information related to mental health crises. First, crises are defined. Then, I provide examples of how these can be related to purposeful danger to self, danger to others, or impairment to the point of danger to self or others, even without intention. We also discuss management of crises and potential interventions to restore a person's level of functioning after the crisis subsides. Finally, we look at some social and cultural elements that can be useful when managing mental health crises within the Mexican American population. The content of this chapter is meant to create awareness of crisis management and to assist in developing culturally sensitive tools or strategies to assist Mexican American clients experiencing a crisis. In the next and last chapter of this book, we look at potential future considerations for the Mexican American population.

Chapter 12

Future Considerations

As I was completing the last few chapters of this book, some of my students asked me about the project. After hearing the rationale for the origin of this book, they asked, "So, what are you going to do now?"

I had been so absorbed by this process that I had not thought about that. Since I have continued working in clinical settings as I finished this book, I had to take a step back and look around me. What I see is a significant shortage of mental health providers, which could make a great impact in this society. If you look at the number of psychologists in Austin, Texas, for example, you would find enough clinicians to work with the majority of people who need psychological services. Unfortunately, that is not always the case, as in the location where I currently practice, South Texas.

After considering that, I knew the answer to my students' question. Now, we begin to make a difference. We begin to apply what I consider to be essential to quality services for Mexican Americans and other culturally disadvantaged groups. The question is, how do we accomplish this?

Like every process and every project, this one has come to the end. As I worked on this manuscript, I realized how much information is out there about Mexican Americans and psychological services. Unfortunately, including all that information in a single project would require several volumes, particularly if we focus on the information that would be useful for clinicians who have not been as exposed to this population. However, I have included information in this book with the intent to provide a core and assist clinicians in becoming culturally competent to work with the Mexican American population.

FROM GENERAL TO SPECIFIC

Before submerging in areas of great need that require adjustments and further considerations, it is important to look at the general social obstacles Mexican Americans face as members of society in the United States.

As covered in previous chapters, the Mexican American population is at a disadvantage compared with other ethnic and cultural groups. The majority do not have higher education degrees, and the rate of those who do is lower than other minority groups; 15.5 percent of Hispanics who are at least 25 years old have a bachelor's degree compared with 36.2 percent of non-Hispanic whites, 22.5 percent of African Americans, and 53.9 percent of Asians (Ryan and Bauman, 2016).

Lower education levels can contribute to an inability to create and promote positive social change. There is nothing wrong with having scholar-practitioners from different ethnic and cultural backgrounds to help the Mexican American population. However, it would certainly be advantageous if more Mexican Americans obtained university degrees to promote change and positive impact within this group.

Stigma and negative attitudes toward mental health and mental illness among Mexican Americans is another problem clinicians who work with this population face. Some Mexican Americans may be more willing to seek assistance from a primary care physician than a specialist in mental health (Leung, LaChapelle, Scinta, and Olvera, 2014). To complicate things further, when the person who suffers from a mental illness accepts it and acknowledges the need for treatment, there may be a shortage of providers where the person resides, making it impossible to receive the treatment required.

GENERAL MENTAL HEALTH TREATMENT FOR MEXICAN AMERICANS

Family members residing in a rural area of Mexico told me about a man in their community they call *el loco*. This man, they reported, "is not all there." After exploring what they meant, it seemed the person is disorganized, may suffer from hallucinations (i.e., seems to have conversations with someone who is not there), and may suffer from delusions, as there are times when he says he is God. Because he is not aggressive and everyone in the community knows him, no one is not concerned about him, and the community just moves on with their daily lives. Instead of being afraid of this man, they have embraced him as a different and strange member of the community. This, of course, would not be the case if the man was aggressive or had engaged in criminal behavior.

I share this story to give a general image of how some people in Mexican communities may perceive individuals who suffer from some sort of psychopathology. Mexican Americans may share this approach and perspective to mental illness because of a lack of information about mental illness and mental health. It is not uncommon for people to look for normal explanations for abnormal behavior that may indicate mental illness and to deny the possibility that a loved one may suffer from a mental illness, which can hinder the therapeutic process.

BECOMING A CULTURALLY COMPETENT PRACTITIONER: GOING AGAINST THE CULTURE OF PSYCHOLOGY

Over the years, significant and numerous changes in the field of psychology have taken place that have shaped it into what it is now. For example, there are now more women in graduate psychology programs than men, which was not even conceivable when the field was created because it was predominantly governed and practiced by men. Several changes have also contributed to making psychology a more inclusive and effective profession. Regarding multiculturalism, we have seen the emergence of a new perspective of mental health and psychology thanks to the work of pioneers such as Derald Wing Sue. However, a lot of work still remains to be done to assist the field in a better understanding and practice toward cultural and ethnic minorities, including the Mexican American.

The question many scholars and practitioners ask is, what needs to be different and how can we accomplish the required changes? These are complex questions that involve a variety of factors. First, it is important to recognize that the field of psychology requires further exploration of the Mexican American population. Having general information about people who consider themselves Latino or Hispanic may not be enough for offering quality services to Mexican Americans. Some of the issues discussed in this book, such as the need for more psychological instruments for Spanish-speaking Mexican Americans, represent areas that need to be further explored. The changes in the field could be more effective if they occurred both at a micro- and a macrolevel. Practitioners can apply some of the information in this book to promote change. Then administrators, scholars, and researchers may be able to propose changes and apply them at a more general level.

Academic programs across the country promote considerations of cultural characteristics of Mexican Americans. Programs of immersion in which graduate students are asked to live in Spanish-speaking countries, including Mexico, for a semester or a year are available. Other programs offer bilingual training. One way to promote change that would benefit

Mexican Americans is to continue expanding these programs and to create new ones.

APPLIED MEXICAN AMERICAN PSYCHOLOGY

Once more scholarly information is utilized to promote positive change, it is up to the practitioners, academics, and others involved in the field to actively apply this information. It would not be useful if the information was there, but never utilized to promote change that would improve the quality of life and level of care of Mexican Americans. There are different ways to apply this information.

One of the most important interventions to assist the Mexican American population is psychoeducational sessions in which people can be informed about mental illness. Such sessions would be particularly effective whenever there is denial. They could also increase the likelihood that a person can be appropriately treated by acknowledging the presence of a mental disorder and then providing treatment as early as possible.

Conducting community health and outreach activities can be the best way to share information and to provide the necessary tools for people to seek help, such as awareness of mental health community resources.

ADVOCACY

Psychologists, counselors, psychiatrists, and other mental health professionals need to take on different roles to assist their clients. Sometimes these professions have to do more than offer mental health treatment; they have to become advocates for their clients or patients. Because of the lack of mental health resources for Mexican Americans, as mentioned, it is not uncommon to find a shortage of people who can defend and actively advocate for some underprivileged populations, including Mexican Americans. One of the best ways to assist Mexican American clients is by providing information and assisting in breaking down stereotypes and inaccurate perceptions about mental health and mental illness. However, there are many other things professionals from different settings can do to successfully advocate for this population.

THE ROLE OF SCHOLARS, PRACTITIONERS, AND EDUCATORS

Scholars can continue to write and conduct research about the Mexican American population. Although much clinical, theoretical, and demographic information pertaining to Mexican Americans is available, numerous things still are not known in the field and require exploration. The best example of this, as discussed in Chapter 10, is the lack of psychological resources for some Mexican American clients. Even though Mexican Americans raised in the United States who have been part of its society for most, if not all, of their lives can participate in some psychological instruments, there are those individuals who have not completely assimilated, and these psychological tools may be conflictive and inaccurate. Especially with Spanish-speaking Mexican Americans, it is important to know which tools may be used and which may not be appropriate. This issue can be addressed by having more instruments and by continuing to expand the general body of knowledge in this area.

As mental health practitioners, it is possible to advocate for Mexican American clients by ensuring that a level of capacity and competency exists in order to offer quality mental health services to this population. Reading a book or attending a seminar that addresses some topics that may surround the Mexican American population may not fully prepare a person to become culturally sensitive and competent. Nevertheless, it guides the practitioner in the right direction, as the first step to promote positive change is to identify gaps and areas that need to be developed to reach an optimal level of competency.

As educators, it is important to transmit to future practitioners the idea of advocacy and to promote quality care in the mental health realm. If the level of care that has been given to some Mexican Americans by certain practitioners who were not trained in multicultural aspects of treatment is poor, lacking, and culturally insensitive, then it is the responsibility of those educators who are aware of these issues to break the cycle of transmitting ineffective or counterproductive approaches to mental health. It is important not only to transmit the information that speaks about how to offer quality mental health services to this population, but also to encourage students to be aware of the areas that require further research and exploration.

Another important item to consider is the role of and the merging of disciplines that form part of the mental health field. Practitioners can be psychologists, psychiatrists, counselors, therapists, educators, and researchers, among other professions. One of the things that can facilitate the push for better services for Mexican Americans is the constant and clear collaboration among these disciplines. Especially in areas where there is a significant shortage of providers, it is beneficial for clients to witness such collaborations because clients would be more likely to receive some sort of intervention. Furthermore, available information from various disciplines may not always be easily shared because of legal and professional constraints (e.g., each discipline is governed by different state boards and state, regional, and national organizations).

BE INCLUSIVE

One of the objectives of this project has been to create consciousness and sensitivity regarding the Mexican American population. This includes being aware of this population's different characteristics. For example, a first-generation Mexican American will have different characteristics when compared to second- or third-generation Mexican Americans. Some of these differences may include language (Spanish versus Spanglish) or social and cultural practices (seeking out services through a family doctor versus going to a folk healer). Being aware of these characteristics can allow the practitioner to offer more effective interventions, with a better understanding of the client. To assume that Mexican American clients have the same characteristics would be a mistake, as there are several types of variables that make every Mexican American client unique. Then again, this is a perspective we try to maintain in the field of psychology. I hope the content of this book will be used as a reference and not as a tool to develop a schema of how every Mexican American client would look.

POLICY

Another way to promote change in the mental health system is through policy. By providing information and evidence that shows the nature of the problem, it is possible to encourage legislators at the state and federal levels to make informed decisions when changing policies and laws. To foster this change, however, it is crucial to be aware of the limitations of available information and to provide accurate data in order to properly inform decision makers.

FINAL THOUGHTS

When I first thought of the concept of this book, I never imagined how complicated it would be to include all of what I considered the most important and relevant information about Mexican American psychology. There is still a lot of information that was not included in this book because this work would require several volumes. My hope is that readers become interested in wanting to do more research for future projects.

Reflecting on the previous 11 chapters, I encourage you to consider the content of this book not only as individual and independent pieces of information, but as a combination of essential information that, when viewed as a whole, can educate and motivate practitioners working with Mexican American clients to offer quality services while maintaining sensitivity toward the specific and particular needs of this population.

Additionally, I hope this project encourages others not only to do further projects about this topic, but also to conduct similar projects about other ethnic or cultural minority groups. Having as much information as possible about these groups can only help in the provision of quality mental health and psychological services which are culturally sensitive and effective for these minorities.

References

Abraído-Lanza, A. F., M. T. Chao, and K. R. Flórez. 2005. "Do healthy behaviors decline with greater acculturation? Implications for the Latino mortality paradox." *Social Science & Medicine* 61: 1243–1255. doi:10.1016/j.socscimed 2005.01.016.

Adair, J. G. 1999. "Indigenisation of psychology: The concept and its practical implementation." *Applied Psychology: An International Review* 48(4): 403–418. doi:10.1080/026999499377385.

Allwood, C. M., and J. W. Berry. 2006. "Origins and development of indigenous psychologies: An international analysis." *International Journal of Psychology* 41(4): 243–268. doi:10.1080/00207590544000013.

Alviso, R. 2011. "What is a corridor? Musical analysis and narrative function." *Studies in Latin American Popular Culture* 29: 58–79.

American Psychiatric Association, *Diagnostic and Statistical Manual of Mental Disorders* (5th ed., text rev.). Washington, DC: Author, 2013.

Anastasi, A., and S. Urbina. *Psychological Testing* (7th ed.). Upper Saddle River, NJ: Prentice Hall, 1997.

Anderson, C., H. Zhao, C. R. Daniel, A. Hromi-Fiedler, Q. Dong, K. Y. Elhor Gbito, X. Wu, and W. Chow. 2016. "Acculturation and diabetes risk in the Mexican American mano a mano cohort." *American Journal of Public Health* 106(3): 547–549.

Applewhite, S. 1995. "Curanderismo: Demystifying the health beliefs and practices of elderly Mexican Americans." *Health & Social Work* 20(4): 247–253. Retrieved from http://www.naswpress.org/publications/journals/hsw.html

Archer, J. 2004. "Sex differences in aggression in real-world settings: A meta-analytic review." *Review of General Psychology* 8(4): 291–322.

Ardonio, G. n.d. "Batería Woodcock-Muñoz." *Facultad de Psicología, UCUDAL.* Retrieved from http://www.scielo.edu.uy/pdf/cp/v3n2/v3n2a13.pdf

Armillas, P. 1971. "Gardens on swamps." *Science* 174(4010): 653–661.

Arnett, J. J. 2008. "The neglected 95%: Why American psychology needs to become less American." *American Psychologist* 63: 602–614. doi:10.1037/0003-066X .63.7.602.

Aviera, A. n.d. "Culturally sensitive and creative therapy with Latino clients." *California Psychological Association Articles.* Retrieved from http://www .apadivisions.org/division-31/publications/articles/california/aviera.pdf

Awad, G. H. 2010. "The impact of acculturation and religious identification on perceived discrimination for Arab/Middle Eastern Americans." *Cultural Diversity and Ethnic Minority Psychology* 16(1): 59–67. http://dx.doi.org/10.1037 /a0016675

Baer, R. D., and M. Bustillo. 1993. "Susto and Mal de Ojo among Florida farmworkers: Emic and etic perspectives." *Medical Anthropology Quarterly, New Series* 7(1): 90–100.

Baer, R. D., and M. Bustillo. 1998. "Caida de mollera among children of Mexican migrant workers: Implications for the study of folk illnesses." *Medical Anthropology Quarterly, New Series* 12(2): 241–249.

Baer, R. D., S. C. Weller, J. G. De Alba Garcia, M. Glazer, R. Trotter, L. Pachter, and R. Klein. 2003. "A cross-cultural approach to the study of the folk illness *nervios*." *Culture, Medicine and Psychiatry* 27: 315–337.

Behnke, A. O., B. A. Taylor, and J. R. Parra-Cardona. 2008. "'I hardly understand English, but . . .': Mexican origin fathers describe their commitment as fathers despite the challenges of immigration." *Journal of Comparative Family Studies* 39: 187–205.

Berdahl, T. A., and R. A. Torres Stone. 2009. "Examining Latino differences in mental healthcare use: The roles of acculturation and attitudes towards healthcare." *Community Mental Health Journal* 45(5): 393–403. doi:10.1007/ s10597-009-9231-6.

Berger, K. S., *Invitation to the Life Span* (3rd ed.). New York: Worth, 2016.

Bermúdez-Parsai, M., J. L. Mullins Geiger, F. F. Marsiglia, and D. V. Coonrod, 2012. "Acculturation and health care utilization among Mexican heritage women in the United States." *Maternal & Child Health Journal* 16: 1173–1179.

Bernard, H. R., *Research Methods in Anthropology: Qualitative and Quantitative Approaches* (4th ed.). New York: Altamira Press, 2006.

Berry, J. W., "Preface." In *Handbook of Cross-Cultural Psychology, Vol 1: Theory and Method* (2nd ed.), edited by J. W. Berry, Y. H. Poortinga, and J. Pandey, x–xv. Boston, MA: Allyn and Bacon, 1997.

Berry, J. W. 2000. "Cross-cultural psychology: A symbiosis of cultural and comparative approaches." *Asian Journal of Social Psychology* 3: 197–205. doi:10.1111/1467-839X.00064.

Berry, J. W. 2001. "A psychology of immigration." *Journal of Social Issues* 57(3): 615–631. doi:10.1111/0022-4537.00231.

Berry, J. W., "Conceptual approaches to acculturation." In *Acculturation: Advances in Theory, Measurement, and Applied Research*, edited by K. M. Chun, P. Balls Organista, and M. Gerardo, 17–37. Washington, DC: American Psychological Association, 2003.

Berry, J. W., and U. Kim, "The way ahead: From indigenous psychologies to a universal psychology." In *Indigenous Psychologies: Research and Experience in Cultural Context*, edited by J. W Berry and U. Kim, 277–280. Newbury Park, CA: Sage Publications, 1993.

Borges, G., C. Rafful, D. J. Tancredi, N. Saito, S. Aguilar-Gaxiola, M. E. Medina-Mora, and J. Breslau. 2013. "Mexican immigration to the U.S., the occurrence of violence and the impact of mental disorders." *Revista Brasileira de Psiquiatria* 35: 161–168.

Bruner, J. 2005. "Cultural psychology and its functions." *Constructivism in the Human Sciences* 10: 53–63.

Buckingham, D. N., K. M. Mackor, R. M. Miller, N. N. Pullman, K. N. Molloy, C. C. Grisby, *et al.* 2013. "Comparing the cognitive screening tools: MMSE and SLUMS." *PURE Insights* 2(3). http://digitalcommons.wou.edu/pure/vol2/iss1/3

Calnek, E. E. 1972. "Settlement pattern and chinampa agriculture at Tenochtitlan." *American Antiquity* 37: 104–115.

Carranza, F. D., S. You, V. Chhuon, and C. Hudley. 2009. "Mexican American adolescents academic achievement and aspirations: The role of perceived parental educational involvement, acculturation, and self-esteem." *Adolescence* 44(174): 313–333.

Carrasco, D. 1995. "Give me some skin: The charisma of the Aztec warrior." *History of Religions* 35(1): 1–26.

Castro, R., and E. Eroza. 1998. "Research notes on social order and subjectivity: Individuals' experience of susto and fallen fontanelle in a rural community in central Mexico." *Culture, Medicine, and Psychiatry* 22(2): 203–230.

Cavazos Vela, J., A. S. Lenz, G. S. Sparrow, S. L. Gonzalez, and K. Hinojosa. 2015. "Humanistic and positive psychology factors as predictors of Mexican American adolescents' vocational outcome expectations." *Journal of Professional Counseling: Practice, Theory, and Research* 42(1): 16–28.

Chalfin, A. 2014. "What is the contribution of Mexican immigration to U.S. crime rates? Evidence from rainfall shocks in Mexico." *American Law and Economics Review* 16(1): 220–268.

Chaudry, A., R. Capps, J. M. Pedroza, R. M. Castañeda, R. Santos, and M. M. Scott. 2010. "Facing our future: Children in the aftermath of immigration enforcement." The Urban Institute. http://www.urban.org/UploadedPDF/412020_FacingOurFuture_nal.pdf

Chehil, S., and S. Kutcher. 2012. *Suicide Risk Management: A Manual for Health Professionals* (2nd ed.). Hoboken, NJ: Wiley-Blackwell.

"Chicana/o." *Oxford English Dictionary* (2nd ed.), 104–105. Oxford: Oxford University Press, 1989.

"Chilango." *Merriam-Webster Online Dictionary–Spanish Central*, 2015. http://www .spanishcentral.com/translate/chilango

Clark, C., and C. Burnett. 2010. "Upward social mobility through women's soccer." *African Journal of Physical Health Education, Recreation and Dance* 16(4): 141–154.

Coe, M. D., and R. Koontz, *Mexico: From the Olmecs to the Aztecs*. New York: Thames & Hudson, 2002.

Comas-Díaz, L. 1998. "Ethnic conflict and the psychology of liberation in Guatemala, Peru, and Puerto Rico." *American Psychologist* 53: 778–792.

Comas-Díaz, L. 2006. "Latino healing: The integration of ethnic psychology into psychotherapy." *Psychotherapy: Theory, Research, Practice, Training* 43(4): 436–453.

Corona Cadena, R. I. 2010. "Los mecanismos miméticos de reproducción de la violencia vistos a través de los narco-corridos." *Universitas Philosophica* 55(27): 221–229.

Cuellar, I., B. Arnold, and R. Maldonado. 1995. "Acculturation Rating Scale for Mexican Americans-II: A revision of the original ARSMA scale." *Hispanic Journal of Behavioral Sciences* 17(3): 275–304.

Davila, M., S. L. McFall, and D. Cheng. 2009. "Acculturation and depressive symptoms among pregnant and postpartum Latinas." *Maternal and Child Health Journal* 13: 318–325. doi:10.1007/s10995-008-0385-6.

Davis, R. E., K. Resnicow, and M. P. Couper. 2011. "Survey response styles, acculturation, and culture among a sample of Mexican American adults." *Journal of Cross-Cultural Psychology* 42(7): 1219–1236.

Dean, W. R., J. R. Sharkey, and J. S. John. 2011. "*Pulga* (flea market) contributions to the retail food environment of *colonias* in the South Texas border region." *Journal of the American Dietetic Association* 111(5): 705–510. doi:10.1016/j .jada.2011.02.009.

Del Castillo, R. G., *The Treaty of Guadalupe Hidalgo*. Norman, OK: University of Oklahoma Press, 1992.

Del Castillo, R. G., and A. De Leon, *North to Aztlan: A History of Mexican Americans in the United States*. New York: Twayne Publishers, 1997.

Diaz, P., D. S. Saenz, and V. S. Y. Kwan. 2011. "Economic dynamics and changes in attitudes toward undocumented Mexican immigrants in Arizona." *Analyses of Social Issues and Public Policy* 11(1): 300–313.

Dotson-Blake, K. P. 2010. "Learning from each other: A portrait of family-school-community partnerships in the United States and Mexico." *Professional School Counseling* 14(1): 101–114.

Draguns, J. G., "Universal and cultural threads in counseling individuals." In *Counseling Across Cultures* (6th ed.), edited by P. Pedersen, J. Draguns, W. Lonner, and J. Trimble, 21–36. Thousand Oaks, CA: Sage Publications, 2008.

Dumitrescu, D. 2014. "English-Spanish code-switching in literary texts: Is it still Spanglish as we know it?" *Hispania* 97(3): 357–359.

Durant, T., J. Mercy, M. Kresnow, T. Simon, L. Potter, and W. R. Haniniond. 2006. "Racial differences in hopelessness as a risk factor for a nearly lethal suicide attempt." *Journal of Black Psychology* 32(3): 285–302.

Durão, A. M. S., and M. C. B. De Mello e Souza. 2006. "Cotidiano de portadores de esquizofrenia, após uso de um antipsicótico atípico e acompanhamento em grupo: Visão do familiar." *Revista Latino-Americana de Enfermagem* 14(4): 586–592.

Ek, L. D., P. Sánchez, and P. D. Quijada Cerecer. 2013. "Linguistic violence, insecurity, and work: Language ideologies of Latina/o bilingual teacher candidates in Texas." *International Multilingual Research Journal* 7: 197–219.

Ember, C. R., M. Ember, and P. N. Peregrine, *Cultural Anthropology* (14th ed.). Upper Saddle River, NJ: Pearson, 2014.

Emery, R. E., R. K. Otto, and W. T. O'Donohue. 2005. "A critical assessment of child custody evaluations: Limited science and a flawed system." *Psychological Science in the Public Interest* 6(1): 1–29.

Englander, K., C. Yáñez, and X. Barney. 2012. "Doing science within a culture of Machismo and Marianismo." *Journal of International Woman's Studies* 13(3): 65–85.

Ennis, S. R., M. Rios-Vargas, and N. G. Albert. 2011. "The Hispanic Population: 2010. 2010 Census Briefs." *United States Census Bureau.* http://www.census.gov/prod/cen2010/briefs/c2010br-04.pdf

Erard, R. E. 2009. "The paradox of indiscriminate multiculturalism." *American Psychologist* 64(6): 564. doi:10.1037/a0016089.

Erskine, R. G., J. P. Moursund, and R. I. Trautmann, *Beyond Empathy: A Therapy of Contact-in-Relationship.* New York: Brunner-Routledge, 1999.

Espenshade, T., and K. Hempstead. 1996. "Contemporary American attitudes toward U.S. immigration." *The International Migration Review* 30(2): 535–570. doi:10.2307/2547393. Retrieved from http://www.jstor.org/stable/2547393

Faudree, P. 2015. "What is an indigenous author?: Minority authorship and the politics of voice in Mexico." *Anthropological Quarterly*, 88(1): 5.

Fisher, C. B., *Decoding the Ethics Code: A Practical Guide for Psychologists.* Thousand Oaks, CA: Sage Publications, 2003.

Frank, R. 1989. "The codex Cortés: Inscribing the conquest of Mexico." *Dispositio* 14: 187–211. Retrieved from http://www.jstor.org/stable/41491359

Gallo, S., H. Link, E. Allard, S. Wortham, and K. Mortimer. 2014. "Conflicting ideologies of Mexican immigrant English across levels of schooling." *International Multilingual Research Journal* 8: 124–140.

Garcia, C., and E. Saewyc. 2007. "Perceptions of mental health among recently immigrated Mexican adolescents." *Issues in Mental Health Nursing* 28(1): 37–54.

Garcia, M. A., J. L. Angel, R. J. Angel, C. T. Chiu, and J. Melvin. 2015. "Acculturation, gender, and active life expectancy in the Mexican-origin population." *Journal of Aging and Health* 27(7): 1247–1265.

Gentsch, K., and D. S. Massey. 2011. "Labor market outcomes for legal Mexican immigrants under the new regime of immigration enforcement." *Social Science Quarterly* 92(3): 875–893.

Gerst, K., M. Al-Ghatrif, H. A. Beard, R. Samper-Ternent, and K. S. Markides. 2010. "High depressive symptomatology among older community-dwelling Mexican Americans: The impact of immigration." *Aging & Mental Health* 14(3): 347–354.

Gerst, K., P. Y. Miranda, K. Eschbach, K. M. Sheffield, M. K. Peek, and K. S. Markides. 2011. "Protective neighborhoods: Neighborhood proportion of Mexican Americans and depressive symptoms in very old Mexican Americans." *Journal of the American Geriatrics Society* 59: 353–358.

Ghazal, R. J. 2013. "Measuring ethnicity with U.S. Census data: Implications for Mexicans and Arabs." *Population Research & Policy Review* 32:611–631. doi:10.1007/s11113-013-9286-5.

Gibson, C., and K. Jung. 2002. "Historical census statistics on population totals by race, 1790 to 1990, and by Hispanic origin, 1970 to 1990, for the United States, regions, divisions, and states." *U.S. Census Bureau.* http://mapmaker .rutgers.edu/REFERENCE/Hist_Pop_stats.pdf

Gil de Zúñiga, H., T. Correa, and S. Valenzuela. 2012. "Selective exposure to cable news and immigration in the U.S.: The relationship between FOX News, CNN, and attitudes toward Mexican immigrants." *Journal of Broadcasting & Electronic Media* 56(4): 597–615.

Glazer, M., R. D. Baer, S. C. Weller, J. E. Garcia de Alba, and S. W. Liebowitz. 2004. "Susto and soul loss in Mexicans and Mexican Americans." *Cross-Cultural Research* 38(3): 270–288.

Gonzales, N. A., L. E. Dumka, R. E. Millsap, A. Gottschall, D. B. McClain, J. J. Wong, et al. 2012. "Randomized trial of a broad preventive intervention for Mexican American adolescents." *Journal of Consulting and Clinical Psychology* 80(1): 1–16.

Gonzalez, H. M., W. Tarraf, and M. N. Haan. 2011. "The metabolic syndrome, biomarkers, and the acculturation-health relationship among older Mexican Americans." *Journal of Aging and Health* 23(7): 1101–1115.

Gonzalez-Barrera, A. and M. H. Lopez. 2013. "A demographic portrait of Mexican-origin Hispanics in the United States." *Pew Research Center*, Feb 16. http:// www.pewhispanic.org/2013/05/01/a-demographic-portrait-of-mexican -origin-hispanics-in-the-united-states/#fn-18153-1

Gorman, B. K., J. Ghazal Read, and P. M. Krueger. 2010. "Gender, acculturation, and health among Mexican Americans." *Journal of Health and Social Behavior* 51(4): 440–457.

Gragg, J. B., and C. M. Wilson. 2011. "Mexican American family's perceptions of the multirelational influences on their adolescent's engagement in substance use treatment." *The Family Journal: Counseling and Therapy for Couples and Families* 19(3): 299–306.

Graves, T. 1967. "Psychological acculturation in a tri-ethnic community." *South-Western Journal of Anthropology* 23: 337–350.

Greenfield, P. M. 2000. "Three approaches to the psychology of culture: Where do they come from? Where can they go?" *Asian Journal of Social Psychology* 3: 223–240. doi:10.1111/1467-839X.00066.

Groth-Marnat, G. *Handbook of Psychological Assessment* (4th ed.). Hoboken, NJ: John Wiley & Sons, 2003.

Grzywacz, J. G., P. Rao, A. Gentry, A. Marín, and T. A. Arcury. 2009. "Acculturation and conflict in Mexican immigrants' intimate partnerships: The role of women's labor force participation." *Violence Against Women* 15(10): 1194–1212. doi:10.1177/1077801209345144.

Haeffel, G. J., E. D. Thiessen, M. W. Campbell, M. P. Kaschak, and N. M. McNeil. 2009. "Theory, not cultural context, will advance American psychology." *American Psychologist* 64(6): 570–571. doi:10.1037/a0016191.

Hanni, K. D., D. A. Ahn, and M. A. Winkleby. 2013. "Signal detection analysis of factors associated with diabetes among semirural Mexican American adults." *Hispanic Journal of Behavioral Sciences* 35(2): 260–277.

Harner, M. 1977. "The ecological basis for Aztec sacrifice." *American Ethnologist* 4(1): 117–135.

Hayner, N. S., and A. M. Montiel. 1964. "La Ciudad de México: Su estructura ecológica latinoamericana." *Revista Mexicana de Sociología* 26(1): 221–231.

Heath, R. H. 1987. "Constraints on peasant maize production: A case study from Michoacan." *Mexican Studies/Estudios Mexicanos* 3(2): 263–286.

Helms, H. M., A. J. Supple, J. Su, Y. Rodriguez, A. M. Cavanaugh, and N. D. Hengstebeck. 2014. "Economic pressure, cultural adaptation stress, and marital quality among Mexican-origin couples." *Journal of Family Psychology* 28(1): 77–87.

Hicks, F. 1982. "Tetzcoco in the early 16th century: The state, the city, and the 'Calpolli.'" *American Ethnologist* 9(2): 230–249.

Hill, C. E., *Helping Skills: Facilitating Exploration, Insight, and Action* (3rd ed.). Washington, DC: American Psychological Association, 2009.

Hinton, L., E. C. Apesoa-Varano, H. M. González, S. Aguilar-Gaxiola, M. Dwight-Johnson, J. C. Barker, C. Tran, R. Zuniga, and J. Unützer. 2012. "Falling through the cracks: Gaps in depression treatment among older Mexican-origin and white men." *International Journal of Geriatric Psychiatry* 27: 1283–1290.

Hoff, L. A., B. J. Hallisey, and M. Hoff, *People in Crisis: Clinical and Diversity Perspectives* (6th ed.). New York: Routledge, 2009.

Huber, B. R., "Introduction." In *Mesoamerican Healers*, edited by B. R. Huber and A. R. Sandstrom, 1–18. Austin: University of Texas Press, 2001.

Huesmann, L. R., L. D. Eron, and P. W. Yarmel (1987). "Intellectual functioning and aggression." *Journal of Personality and Social Psychology* 52(1): 232–240.

Hwang, K. 2005a. "A philosophical reflection on the epistemology and methodology of indigenous psychologies." *Asian Journal of Social Psychology* 8(5): 5–17. doi:10.1111/j.1467-839X.2005.00153.x.

Hwang, K. 2005b. "The third wave of cultural psychology: The indigenous move-ment." *Psychologist* 18(2): 80–83. Retrieved from http://www.thepsychologist .org.uk/

Ingham, J. M. 1971. "Time and space in ancient Mexico: The symbolic dimensions of clanship." *Man. New Series* 6: 615–629.

Ismail, Z., T. K. Rajji, and K. I. Shulman. 2010. "Brief cognitive screening instru-ments: An update." *International Journal of Geriatric Psychiatry* 25: 111–120.

Jiang, M., R. J. Green, T. B. Henley, and W. G. Masten. 2009. "Acculturation in rela-tion to the acquisition of a second language." *Journal of Multilingual and Multicultural Development* 30(6): 481–492. doi:10.1080/01434630903147898.

Jiménez, T. R. 2009. "What different generations of Mexican Americans think about immigration from Mexico." *The American Society of Aging* 32(4): 93–96.

Johnston, M. F., S. Karageorgis, and I. Light. 2013. "Mexican population growth in new U.S. destinations: Testing and developing social capital theories of migration using census data." *Journal of Ethnic and Migration Studies* 39(9): 1479–1505.

Jonsson, C. 2012. "Power and resistance: Language mixing in three Chicano plays." *International Journal of Bilingualism* 18(2): 118–133.

Kaestner, R., and O. Malamud. 2014. "Self-selection and international migration: New evidence from Mexico." *The Review of Economics and Statistics* 96(1): 78–91.

Kao, H. S., and K. An. 2012. "Effect of acculturation and mutuality on family loy-alty among Mexican American caregivers of elders." *Journal of Nursing Schol-arship* 44(2): 111–119.

Keatinge, C., and J. T. Olin, *Rapid Psychological Assessment*. New York: John Wiley & Sons, 1998.

Keegan, L. 2000. "A comparison of the use of alternative therapies among Mexican Americans and Anglo-Americans in the Texas Rio Grande Valley." *Journal of Holistic Nursing* 18(3): 280–295. doi:10.1177/089801010001800308.

Kellogg, S., *Law and the Transformation of Aztec Society, 1500–1700*. Norman, OK: University of Oklahoma Press, 1995.

Kim, H. S., and D. K. Sherman. 2009. "The irony of cultural psychology research." *American Psychologist* 64(6): 564–565. doi:10.1037/a0016680.

King, M. C. 2011. "Mexican women and work on both sides of the U.S.-Mexican border." *American Journal of Economics and Sociology* 70(3): 615–368.

Knight, G. P., D. Vargas-Chanes, and S. H. Losoya. 2009. "Acculturation and encul-turation trajectories among Mexican-American adolescent offenders." *Jour-nal of Research on Adolescence* 19(4): 625–653.

Koocher, G. P., and P. Keith-Spiegel, *Ethics in Psychology: Professional Standards and Cases*. New York: Oxford University Press, 1998.

Kyratzis, A., Y. T. Tang, and S. B. Koymen. 2009. "Codes, code-switching, and context: Style and footing in peer group bilingual play." *Multilingua* 28: 265–290.

Landy, D. 1985. "Review: A syndrome and its meaning." *Science, New Series* 228(4701): 850–851.

Laungani, P. 2002. "Cross-cultural psychology: A handmaiden to mainstream Western psychology." *Counseling Psychology Quarterly* 15(4): 385–397. doi:10.10 80/0951507031000069392.

Lee, C., D. Li, S. Arai, and K. Puntillo. 2009. "Ensuring cross-cultural equivalence in translation of research consents and clinical documents: A systematic process for translating English to Chinese." *Journal of Transcultural Nursing* 77(20): 77–82. Retrieved from http://tcn.sagepub.com

Leidy, M. S., N. G. Guerra, and R. I. Toro. 2010. "Positive parenting, family cohesion, and child social competence among immigrant Latino families." *Journal of Family Psychology* 24(3): 252–260.

Leitão Bautista, M. A., J. Fernandes Filho, and P. M. Silva Dantas. 2007. "The influence intensity of training in a weight loss in soccer." *Fitness & Performance* 6(4): 251–254. Retrieved from http://www.fpjournal.org.br/painel/arquivos /469-8%20Futebol%20Rev%204%202007%20Ingles.pdf

Leo, R. J. 1999. "Competency and the capacity to make treatment decisions: A primer for primary care physicians." *Primary Care Companion of the Journal of Clinical Psychiatry* 1(5): 131–141.

Leon-Portilla, M. *Aztec Thought and Culture.* Norman, OK: University of Oklahoma Press, 1963.

Leung, P., A. R. LaChapelle, A. Scinta, and N. Olvera. 2014. "Factors contributing to depressive symptoms among Mexican Americans and Latinos." *Social Work* 59(1): 42–51.

Levin Rojo, D. A., *Return to Aztlan: Indians, Spaniards, and the Invention of Nuevo México.* Norman, OK: University of Oklahoma Press, 2014.

Lipsicas, C. B., and I. H. Mäkinen. 2010. "Immigration and suicidality in the young." *La Revue Canadienne de Psychiatrie* 55(5): 274–279. Retrieved from http:// publications.cpa-apc.org/browse/sections/0

Lizardi, D., M. A. Oquendo, and R. Graver. 2009. "Clinical pitfalls in the diagnosis of *ataque de nervios*: A case study." *Transcultural Psychiatry* 46(3): 463–486. doi:10.1177/1363461509343090.

Logan, M. H. 1993. "New lines of inquiry on the illness of susto." *Medical Anthropology* 15(2): 189–200.

Lonner, W. J., and J. Adamopoulos, "Culture as antecedent to behavior." In *Handbook of Cross-Cultural Psychology, Vol 1: Theory and Method* (2nd ed.), edited by J. W. Berry, Y. H. Poortinga, and J. Pandey, 43–83. Boston, MA: Allyn and Bacon, 1997.

López, G. 2015. "Hispanics of Mexican origin in the United States, 2013." *Pew Research Center.* Retrieved from http://www.pewhispanic.org/2015/09/15 /hispanics-of-mexican-origin-in-the-united-states-2013

Lutkehaus, N. C. 2008. "Putting 'culture' into cultural psychology: Anthropology's role in the development of Bruner's cultural psychology." *Ethos* 36(1): 46–59. doi:10.1111/j.1548-1352.2008.00003.x.

Malott, K. M., and T. R. Paone. 2013. "Mexican-origin adolescents' exploration of a group experience." *Journal of Creativity in Mental Health* 8: 204–218.

Marín, G., F. Sabogal, B. VanOss Marín, B., F. Otero-Sabogal, and E. J. Pérez-Stable. 1987. "Development of a short acculturation scale for Hispanics." *Hispanic Journal of Behavioral Sciences* 9: 183–205.

Marrs Fuchsel, C. L., S. B. Murphy, and R. Dufresne. 2012. "Domestic violence, culture, and relationship dynamics among immigrant Mexican women." *Journal of Women and Social Work* 27(3): 263–274.

Marsiglia, F. F., S. Kulis, H. Garcia Perez, and M. Bermudez-Parsai. 2011. "Hopelessness, family stress, and depression among Mexican-heritage mothers in the Southwest." *Health & Social Work* 36(1): 7–18.

Marsiglia, F. F., J. L. Nagoshi, M. Parsai, J. M. Booth, and F. González Castro. 2014. "The parent-child acculturation gap, parental monitoring, and substance use in Mexican heritage adolescents in Mexican neighborhoods of the Southwest U.S." *Journal of Community Psychology* 42(5): 530–543.

Martínez-Ramírez, D., M. Rodríguez-Violante, P. González-Latapi, A. Cervantes-Arriaga, A. Camacho-Ordoñez, H. Morales-Briceño, *et al.* 2014. "Comparison of the Montreal Cognitive Assessment and Mini Mental State Examination performance in patients with Parkinson's disease with low educational background." *Research in Neurology: An international Journal* (2014): 1–7.

Martinez-Taboas, A., and G. Bernal. 2000. "Dissociation, psychopathology, and abusive experiences in a nonclinical Latino university student group." *Cultural Diversity and Ethnic Minority Psychology* 6(1): 32–41.

Masel, M. C., B. Howrey, and M. K. Peek. 2011. "The effect of acculturation on frailty among older Mexican Americans." *Journal of Aging and Health* 23(4): 704–713.

Massey, D. S, and C. Capoferro, "The geographic diversification of U.S. immigration." In *New Faces in New Places: The Changing Geography of American Immigration*, edited by M. S. Massey, 25–50. New York: Russell Sage, 2008.

Mattingly, C., N. C. Lutkehaus, and C. J. Throop. 2008. "Bruner's search for meaning: A conversation between psychology and anthropology." *Ethos* 36(1): 1–28. doi:10.1111/j.1548-1352.2008.00001.x.

May, K. M., and L. Rew. 2009. "Mexican American youths' and mothers' explanatory models of diabetes prevention." *Journal for Specialists in Pediatric Nursing* 15(1): 6–15.

McCabe, K., and M. Yeh. 2009. "Parent–child interaction therapy for Mexican Americans: A randomized clinical trial." *Journal of Clinical Child & Adolescent Psychology* 38(5): 753–759.

McDowell, J. H. 2012. "The ballad of narcomexico." *Journal of Folklore Research* 49(3): 249–274.

McGlothlin, H., and M. Killen. 2006. "Intergroup attitudes of European American children attending ethnically homogeneous schools." *Child Development* 77(5): 1375–1386.

Meireles de Pontes, L., and M. S. Cirilo de Sousa. 2009. "Nutritional status and prevalence of metabolic syndrome in amateur soccer players." *Revista Brasileira de Medicina do Esporte* 15(3): 185–189.

Melton, G. B., J. Petrila, N. G. Poythress, C. Slobogin, P. M. Lyons Jr., and R. K. Otto, *Psychological Evaluations for the Courts: A Handbook for Mental Health Professionals and Lawyers* (3rd ed.). New York: Guilford Press, 2007.

Merkin, R. 2015. "The relationship between individualism/collectivism." *Journal of Intercultural Communication* 39(4).

Molina, N. 2011. "Borders, laborers, and radicalized medicalization: Mexican immigration and U.S. public health practices in the 20th century." *Public Health Then and Now* 101(6): 1024–1031.

Moore, J. D., *Visions of Culture: An Introduction to Anthropological Theories and Theorists* (4th ed.). London: Altamira Press, 2012.

Morales, L. S., M. Leng, and J. J. Escarce. 2011. "Risk of cardiovascular disease in first and second generation Mexican-Americans." *Journal of Immigrant Minority Health* 13: 61–68.

Morehart, C. T., and S. Morell-Hart. 2015. "Beyond the ecofact: Toward a social paleoethnobotany in Mesoamerica." *Journal of Archaeological Method and Theory* 22(2): 483–511.

Morello, M. I., H. Madanat, N. C. Crespo, H. Lemus, and J. Elder. 2012. "Associations among parent acculturation, child BMI, and child fruit and vegetable consumption in a Hispanic sample." *Journal of Immigrant and Minority Health* 14: 1023–1029.

Moya Salas, L., C. Ayón, and M. Gurrola. 2013. "Estamos traumados: The effect of anti-immigrant sentiment and policies on the mental health of Mexican immigrant families." *Journal of Community Psychology* 41(8): 1005–1020.

Mundy, B. E. 1998. "Mapping the Aztec capital: The 1524 Nuremberg map of Tenochtitlan, its sources and meanings." *Imago Mundi* 50: 11–33.

Myers, D. G., *Exploring Psychology* (9th ed.). New York: Worth Publishers, 2012.

Mysyk, A. 1998. "Susto: An illness of the poor." *Dialectical Anthropology* 23: 187–202.

Nagayama Hall, G. C., and G. G. Maramba. 2001. "In search of cultural diversity: Recent literature in cross-cultural and ethnic minority psychology." *Cultural Diversity and Ethnic Minority Psychology* 7(1): 12–26. doi:10.1037/1099-9809.7.1.12.

National Alliance on Mental Illness (NAMI)–Minnesota, *Mental Health Crisis Planning: Learn to Recognize, Manage, Prevent and Plan for Your Loved One's Mental Health Crisis.* St. Paul, MN: NAMI, 2010.

National Suicide Prevention Lifeline. www.Suicidepreventionlifeline.org

Nekby, L., M. Rödin, and G. Özcan. 2009. "Acculturation identity and higher education: Is there a trade-off between ethnic identity and education?" *International Migration Review* 43(4): 938–973. doi:10.1111/j.1747-7379.2009.00790.x.

Nieri, T., and M. Bermudez-Parsai. 2014. "Gap or overlap? Parent–child acculturation differences in Mexican immigrant families." *Hispanic Journal of Behavioral Sciences* 36(4): 413–434.

Nortman, D. L., J. Halvas, and A. Rabago. 1986. "A cost-benefit analysis of the Mexican social security administration's family planning program." *Studies in Family Planning* 17(1): 1–6.

Nuccetelli, S. 2001. "'Latinos,' 'Hispanics,' and 'Iberoamericans': Naming or describing?" *The Philosophical Forum* 32(2): 175–188.

O'Donnell, C. R. 2006. "Beyond diversity: Toward a cultural community psychology." *American Journal of Community Psychology* 37(1–2): 1–7. doi:10.1007/s10464-005-9010-7.

O'nell, C. W. 1975. "An investigation of reported 'fright' as a factor in the etiology of susto, 'Magical Fright.'" *Ethos* 3(1): 41–63.

Office of the Surgeon General; Center for Mental Health Services; National Institute of Mental Health, "Mental healthcare for Hispanic Americans." In *Mental Health: Culture, Race, and Ethnicity: A Supplement to Mental Health: A Report of the Surgeon General.* Rockville, MD: Substance Abuse and Mental Health Services Administration (US), 2001.

Oluyomi, A. O., L. W. Whitehead, K. D. Burau, E. Symanski, H. W. Kohl, and M. Bondy. 2014. "Physical activity guideline in Mexican-Americans: Does the built environment play a role?" *Journal of Immigrant and Minority Health* 16: 244–255.

Ortega, A. N., G. Canino, and M. Alegria. 2008. "Lifetime and 12-month intermittent explosive disorder in Latinos." *American Journal of Orthopsychiatry* 78(1): 133–139.

Ortiz de Montellano, B. 1987. "Caida de mollera: Aztec sources for a Mesoamerican disease of alleged Spanish origin." *Ethnohistory* 34(4): 381–399.

Osuna, A. R., and H. R. Navarro. 2008. "Inmigración, estrategias de aculturación y valores laborales: Un estudio exploratorio." *Revista de Psicología del Trabajo y de las Organizaciones* 24(2): 187–202.

Otheguy, R., and N. Stern. 2010. "On so-called Spanish." *International Journal of Bilingualism* 15(1): 85–100.

Ottenheimer, H. J., *The Anthropology of Language: An Introduction to Linguistic Anthropology.* Belmont, CA: Wadsworth Cengage Learning, 2013.

Padilla, A. M., and N. E. Borrero, "The effects of acculturative stress on the Hispanic family." In *Handbook of Multicultural Perspectives on Stress and Coping: Part of the Series: International and Cultural Psychology*, edited by P. T. P. Wong and L. C. J. Wong, 299–317. New York: Springer, 2006.

Palmer, D. K., S. G. Mateus, R. A. Martínez, and K. Henderson. 2014. "Reframing the debate on language separation: Toward a vision for translanguaging pedagogies in the dual language classroom." *The Modern Language Journal* 98(3): 757–772.

Paquet, S. L., and T. Kline. 2009. "Uncovering the psychometric properties of scales measuring individualist and collectivist orientation." *International Journal of Testing* 9: 260–270. doi:10.1080/15305050903106859.

Pardo, Y., C. Weisfeld, E. Hill, and R. B. Slatcher. 2013. "Machismo and marital satisfaction in Mexican American couples." *Journal of Cross-Cultural Psychology* 44(2): 299–315.

Paredes, A., *A Texas–Mexican Cancionero: Folksongs of the Lower Border*. Urbana, IL: University of Illinois Press, 1976.

Paredes, A., *Folklore and Culture On the Texas–Mexican Border*. Austin: University of Texas Press, 1993.

Paredes, A., *With His Pistol in His Hand: A Border Ballad and Its Hero*. Austin: University of Texas Press, 1958.

Peña, F. B., G. Villalobos, M. A. Martinez, A. Sotelo, L. Gil, and A. Delgado-Salinas. 1999. "Use and nutritive value of talet beans, *Amphicarpaea bracteata* (Fabaceae: Phaseoleae) as human food in Puebla, Mexico." *Economic Botany* 53(4): 427–434.

Perez, A. D., "Who is Hispanic? Shades of ethnicity among Latino/a youth." In *Racism in Post-Race America: New Theories, New Directions*, edited by C. A. Gallagher, 17–33. Morrisville, NC: University of North Carolina, 2008.

Pescador, J. J. 2004. "¡Vamos taximaroa! Mexican/Chicano soccer associations and transnational/translocal communities, 1967–2002." *Latino Studies* 2(3): 352–376.

Pescador, J. J., "Los heroes del domingo: Soccer, borders, and social spaces in Great Lakes Mexican communities, 1940–1970." In *Mexican Americans and Sports: A Reader on Athletics and Barrio Life*, edited by J. Iber, and S. O. Regalado, 73–88. College Station, TX: Texas A&M University Press, 2006.

Phinney, J. 1992. "The Multigroup Ethnic Identity Measure: A new scale for use with adolescents and young adults from diverse groups." *Journal of Adolescent Research* 7: 156–176.

Pierce, C., J. Carew, D. Pierce-Gonzalez, and D. Willis, "An experiment in racism: TV commercials." In *Television and Education*, edited by C. Pierce, 62–88. Beverly Hills, CA: Sage Publications, 1978.

Piña-Watson, B., L. G. Castillo, and R. Castillo-Reyes. 2014. "The marianismo beliefs scale: Validation with Mexican American adolescent girls and boys." *Journal of Latina/o Psychology* 2(2): 113–130.

Piña-Watson, B., J. D. Llamas, and A. K. Stevens. 2015. "Attempting to successfully straddle the cultural divide: Hopelessness model of bicultural stress, mental health, and caregiver connection for Mexican descent adolescents." *Journal of Counseling Psychology* 62(4): 670–681.

Piña-Watson, B., L. Ojeda, N. E. Castellon, and M. Dornhecker. 2013. "Familismo, ethnic identity, and bicultural stress as predictors of Mexican American adolescents' positive psychological functioning." *Journal of Latina/o Psychology* 1(4): 204–217.

Porter, E. 2005. "Not on the radar: Illegal immigrants are bolstering social security." *Generations* 29(1): 100–102.

Postma, R. L. 2013. "'¿Porqué leemos esto en la clase de Español?': The politics of teaching literature in Spanglish." *Hispania* 96(3): 442–443.

Purnell, L. D., *Transcultural Health Care: A Culturally Competent Approach* (4th ed.). Philadelphia, PA: F. A. Davis, 2013.

Purnell, L. D., and S. Pontious, "Cultural Competence." In *Multicultural Approaches to Health and Wellness in America, Vol 1: Key Issues and Medical Systems*, edited by R. Gurung, 1–28. Santa Barbara, CA: Praeger, 2014.

Ramirez III, M., N. L. Argueta, and J. R. Grasso. 2013. "Drug trafficking and immigration: Impact on the borderlands culture of South Texas." *Journal of Latina/o Psychology* 1(2): 69–84.

Ramos-Sánchez, L. 2007. "Language switching and Mexican Americans' emotional expression." *Journal of Multicultural Counseling and Development* 35: 154–168.

Ramos-Sánchez, L. 2009. "Counselor bilingual ability, counselor ethnicity, acculturation, and Mexican Americans' perceived counselor credibility." *Journal of Counseling & Development* 87: 331–318.

Rangel, N., V. Loureiro-Rodríguez, and M. I. Moyna. 2015. "'Is that what I sound like when I speak?' Attitudes towards Spanish, English, and code-switching in two Texas border towns." *Spanish in Context* 12(2): 177–198.

Rios Contreras, V. 2014. "The role of drug-related violence and extortion in promoting Mexican migration: Unexpected consequences of a drug war." *Latin American Research Review* 49(3): 199–217.

Roberts, A. R., and A. J. Ottens. 2005. "The seven-stage crisis intervention model: A road map to goal attainment, problem solving, and crisis resolution." *Brief Treatment and Crisis Intervention* 5(4): 329–339

Rodriguez, A. S. 2010–2011. "Why Cesar Chavez led a movement as well as a union." *Harvard Journal of Hispanic Policy* 23: 15–21.

Rodriguez Gutierrez, M. C., and S. Echegoyen Monroy. 2002. "Manejo conservador de los esguinces de tobillo." *Revista de la Facultad de Medicina UNAM* 45(6): 243–244.

Rojas Gonzalez, F. 1945. "El comercio entre los indios de Mexico." *Revista Mexicana de Sociología* 7(1): 123–137.

Romero, M. 2005. "Brown is beautiful." *Law & Society Review* 39(1): 211–234.

Rosas, A. E. 2011. "Breaking the silence: Mexican children and women's confrontation of Bracero family separation, 1942–64." *Gender & History* 23(2): 382–400.

Rossetti, H. C., L. H. Lacritz, C. M. Cullum, and M. F. Weiner. 2011. "Normative data for the Montreal Cognitive Assessment (MoCA) in a population-based sample." *Neurology* 77: 1272–1275.

Rothbaum, F., J. Weisz, M. Pott, K. Miyake, and G. Morelli. 2001. "Deeper into attachment and culture." *American Psychologists* 56(10): 827–829. doi:10.1037/0003-066X.56.10.827.

Rothman, N. C. 2016. "Peopling of the Western hemisphere." *Comparative Civilizations Review* 74: 67–80.

Rothstein, F. A. 1999. "Declining odds: Kinship, women's employment, and political economy in rural Mexico." *American Anthropologist, New Series* 101(3): 579–593.

Rubel, A. J. 1964. "The epidemiology of a folk illness: Susto in Hispanic America." *Ethnology* 3(3): 268–283.

Ryan, C. L., and K. Bauman. 2016. "Educational attainment in the United States: 2015. Population characteristics. Current population reports." *United States Census Bureau.*

Salinas, J. J., H. D. de Heer, L. M. Lapeyrouse, J. M. Heyman, and H. G. Balcázar. 2015. "Insurance status is a greater barrier than income or acculturation to chronic disease screening in the Mexican origin population in El Paso, Texas." *Hispanic Health Care International* 13(4): 197–208.

Sam, D. L., and J. W. Berry. 2010. "Acculturation: When individuals and groups of different cultural backgrounds meet." *Perspectives on Psychological Science* 5(4): 472–481. doi:10.1177/1745691610373075.

Sánchez-Escobedo, P., L. Hollingworth, and A. D. Fina. 2011. "A cross-cultural, comparative study of the American, Spanish, and Mexican versions of the WISC-IV." *TESOL Quarterly* 45(4): 781–792.

Sánchez-Muñoz, A. 2013. "Who soy yo?: The creative use of 'Spanglish' to express a hybrid identity in Chicana/o heritage language learners of Spanish." *Hispania* 96(3): 440–441.

Sandler, A. P., and L. S. Chan. 1978. "Mexican-American folk belief in a pediatric emergency room." *Medical Care* 16(9): 778–784.

Santamaria, A., M. Cubero, and M. L. De la Mata. 2010. "Thinking as action: Theoretical and methodological requirements for cultural psychology." *Theory Psychology* 20(1): 76–101. doi:10.1177/0959354309350244.

Santiago-Rivera, A. L. 2003. "Latinos, value, and family transitions: Practical considerations for counseling." *Journal of Counseling and Human Development* 35: 1–12.

Santrock, J. W., *A Topical Approach to Life-Span Development* (3rd ed.). Boston: McGraw Hill, 2007.

Sarabia, H. 2012. "Perpetual illegality: Results of border enforcement and policies for Mexican undocumented migrants in the U.S." *Analyses of Social Issues and Public Policy* 12(1): 49–67.

Sattler, J. M., *Assessment of Children: Cognitive Applications* (4th ed.). San Diego, CA: Jerome M. Sattler, 2001.

Schlomann, P., S. Hesler, S. Fister, and D. Taft. 2012. "Mexican immigrants' perceptions about changes in diet, physical activity, stress, and health." *Hispanic Health Care International* 10(4): 190–198.

Schofield, T. J., R. D. Parke, Y. Kim, and S. Coltrane. 2008. "Bridging the acculturation gap: Parent–child relationship quality as a moderator in Mexican American families." *Developmental Psychology* 44(4): 1190–1194

Schwartz, S. J., and B. L. Zamboanga. 2008. "Testing Berry's model of acculturation: A confirmatory latent class approach." *Cultural Diversity and Ethnic Minority Psychology* 14(4): 275–285. doi:10.1037/a0012818.

Scupin, R., *Cultural Anthropology: A Global Perspective* (8th ed.). Upper Saddle River, NJ: Pearson, 2012.

Shorris, E., *Latinos: A Biography of the People*. New York: W.W. Norton & Company, 2012.

Shweder, R. A., "Cultural psychology-What is it?" In *Cultural Psychology: Essays on Comparative Human Development*, edited by J. W. Stigler, R. A. Scheder, and G. Herdt, 1–44. Cambridge: Cambridge University Press, 1990.

Silva Gruesz, K. 2012. "Alien speech, incorporated: On the cultural history of Spanish in the U.S." *American Literary History* 25(1): 18–32.

Smith, G. T., N. S. Spillane, and A. M. Annus. 2006. "Implications of an emerging integration of universal and culturally specific psychologies." *Perspectives on Psychological Science* 3(1): 211–233. doi:10.1111/j.1745-6916.2006.00013.x.

Smith, K. M., M. S. Chesin, and E. L. Jeglic. 2014. "Minority college student mental health: Does majority status matter? Implications for college counseling services." *Journal of Multicultural Counseling and Development* 42: 77–92.

Smith, M. E. 1984. "The Aztlan migrations of the Nahuatl chronicles: Myth or history?" *Ethnohistory* 31(3): 153–186.

Smith, M. E., P. Aguirre, C. Heath-Smith, K. Hirst, S. O'Mack, and J. Price. 1989. "Architectural patterns at three Aztec-period sites in Morelos, Mexico." *Journal of Field Archaeology* 16: 185–203.

Smokowski, P. R., and M. L. Bacallao. 2007. "Acculturation, internalizing mental health symptoms, and self-esteem: Cultural experiences of Latino adolescents in North Carolina." *Child Psychiatry and Human Development* 37(3): 273–292. doi:10.1007/s10578-006-0035-4.

Sotomayor-Peterson, M., A. J. Figueredo, D. H. Christensen, and A. R. Taylor. 2012. "Couples' cultural values, shared parenting, and family emotional climate within Mexican American families." *Family Process* 51(2): 218–233.

Spence, M. W. 1967. "The obsidian industry of Teotihuacan." *American Antiquity* 32(4): 507–514.

Stettin, B., J. Geller, K. Ragosta, K. Cohen, and J. Ghowrwal. 2014. "Mental health commitment laws: A survey of the states." *Treatment Advocacy Center*. Retrieved from http://tacreports.org/storage/documents/2014-state-survey-abridged.pdf

Sue, D. W., C. M. Capodilupo, G. C. Torino, J. M. Bucceri, A. M. B. Holder, K. L. Nadal, and M. E. Esquilin. 2007. "Racial microaggressions in everyday life: Implications for clinical practice." *American Psychologist* 62: 271–286.

Sue, D. W., and D. Sue, *Counseling the Culturally Diverse: Theory and Practice* (6th ed.). Hoboken, NJ: John Wiley & Sons, 2012.

Suleiman, L. 2003. "Beyond cultural competence: Language access and Latino civil rights." *Child Welfare* 82(2): 185–200.

Sullivan, M. S., and R. Rehm. 2005. "Mental health of undocumented Mexican immigrants: A review of the literature." *Advances in Nursing Science* 28(3): 240–251.

Szapocznik, J., W. Kurtines, and T. Fernandez. 1980. "Bicultural involvement and adjustment in Hispanic-American youths." *International Journal of Intercultural Relations* 4: 353–365.

Tariq, S. H., N. Tumosa, J. T. Chibnall, M. H. Perry, and J. E. Morley. 2006. "Comparison of the Saint Louis University mental status examination and the mini-mental state examination for detecting dementia and mild neurocognitive disorder—a pilot study." *American Journal of Geriatric Psychiatry* 14(11): 900–910.

Tatar, B. 2010. "Hombres bravos, mujeres bravas: Gender and violence in the Mexican corrido." *Asian Journal of Latin American Studies* 23(4): 83–117.

"Tejano." *Webster's New World College Dictionary*, 1471. Springfield, MA: Merriam-Webster, 2007.

Tharp, R. G. 2007. "A perspective on unifying culture and psychology: Some philosophical and scientific issues." *Journal of Theoretical and Philosophical Psychology* 27(2): 213–233. doi:10.1037/h0091294.

Toomey, R. B., A. J. Umaña-Taylor, D. R. Williams, E. Harvey-Mendoza, L. B. Jahromi, and K. A. Updegraff. 2014. "Impact of Arizona's SB 1070 immigration law on utilization of health care and public assistance among Mexican-origin adolescent mothers and their mother figures." *American Journal of Public Health* 104(S1): S28–S32.

Torres, L. 2010. "Predicting levels of Latino depression: Acculturation, acculturative stress and coping." *Cultural Diversity and Ethnic Minority Psychology* 16(2): 256–263. doi:10.1037/a0017357.

Torres, M. (2004). "To the margins and back: The high cost of being Latina in America." *Journal of Latinos & Education* 3(2): 123–141.

Torres, M., D. Parra-Medina, and A. Johnson. 2008. "Rural hospitals and Spanish speaking patients with limited English proficiency." *Journal of Healthcare Management* 53(2): 107–120.

Tousignant, M. 1982. "Emotions and psychopathology: An aboriginal theory." *Acta Psiquiátrica y Psicológica de America Latina* 27(3): 194–199.

Tovar, M., "Mexican-American medicine: History, roots, and key maladies." In *Multicultural Approaches to Health and Wellness in America, Vol 1: Key Issues and Medical Systems*, edited by R. Gurung, 259–280. Santa Barbara, CA: Praeger, 2014.

Train, R. W. 2013. "Becoming bilingual, becoming ourselves: Archival memories of Spanglish in early Californian epistolary texts." *Hispania* 96(3): 438–439.

Triandis, H. C. 2000. "Dialectics between cultural and cross-cultural psychology." *Asian Journal of Social Psychology* 3: 185–195. doi:10.1111/1467-839X.00063.

Trillo, A. 2004. "Somewhere between Wall Street and El Barrio: Community college and the children of Latino immigrants." *Conference Papers—American Sociological Association.*

Trotter II, R. T. 1991. "A survey of four illnesses and their relationship to intracultural variation in a Mexican-American community." *American Anthropologist* 93(1): 115–125.

Trotter II, R. T., and J. A. Chavira, *Curanderismo: Mexican American Folk Healing* (2nd ed.). Athens, GA: University of Georgia Press, 1997.

Ulin, R. 2007. "Revisiting cultural relativism: Old prospects for a new cultural critique." *Anthropological Quarterly* 803: 820.

United States Census Bureau. 2013 "Hispanic Origin." *United States Census Bureau.* July 25, 2013. http://www.census.gov/topics/population/hispanic-origin/about.html

U.S. Department of Health and Human Services. Substance Abuse and Mental Health Services Administration, Center for Mental Health Services. 2009. *Practice Guidelines: Core Elements for Responding to Mental Health Crises.* HHS Pub. No. SMA-09-4427. Rockville, MD: Center for Mental Health Services, Substance Abuse and Mental Health Services Administration.

Valencia-García, D., J. M. Simoni, M. Alegría, and D. T. Takeuchi. 2012. "Social capital, acculturation, mental health, and perceived access to services among Mexican American women." *Journal of Latina/o Psychology* 1(S): 78–89.

Vasquez, J. 2005. "Perceptions of racism and consolidation of identity among Mexican Americans." *Conference Papers—American Sociological Association.*

Vela, B., "Edcouch-Elsa walk-out." *Valley Delta News,* June 14, 2014.

Vella, C. A., D. Ontiveros, R. Y. Zubia, and J. O. Bader. 2011. "Acculturation and metabolic syndrome risk factors in young Mexican and Mexican-American women." *Journal of Immigrant and Minority Health* 13: 119–126.

Vijayaraghavan, M., G. He, P. Stoddard, and D. Schillinger. 2010. "Blood pressure control, hypertension, awareness, and treatment in adults with diabetes in the United States-Mexico border region." *Revista Panamericana de Salud Publica* 28(3): 164–173.

Villalba, J. A., N. N. Ivers, and A. B. Ohlms. 2010. "*Cuento* group work in emerging rural Latino communities: Promoting personal-social development of Latina/o middle school students of Mexican heritage." *Journal for Specialists in Group Work* 35(1): 23–43.

Vincent, D. 2009. "Culturally tailored education to promote lifestyle change in Mexican Americans with type 2 diabetes." *Journal of the Academy of Nurse Practitioners* 21: 520–527.

Wald, E., *Narcocorrido: A Journey into the Music of Drugs, Guns, and Guerrillas.* New York: HarperCollins, 2002.

Waldstein, A. 2008. "Diaspora and health? Traditional medicine and culture in a Mexican migrant community." *International Migration* 46(5): 95–117. doi:10.1111/j.1468-2435.2008.00490.x.

Warren, R., and D. Kerwin. 2015. "Beyond DAPA and DACA: Revisiting legislative reform in light of long-term trends in unauthorized immigration to the United States." *Journal on Migration and Human Security* 3(1): 80–108.

Weller, S. C., and R. D. Baer. 2001. "Intra- and intercultural variation in the definition of five illnesses: AIDS, diabetes, the common cold, empacho, and mal de ojo." *Cross-Cultural Research: The Journal of Comparative Social Science* 35(2): 201–226.

Weller, S. C., L. M. Pachter, R. T. Trotter II, and R. D. Baer. 1993. "Empacho in four Latino groups: A study of intra- and intercultural variation in beliefs." *Medical Anthropology* 15: 109–136.

Wilkerson, J. A., N. Yamawaki, and S. D. Downs. 2009. "Effects of husbands' migration on mental health and gender role ideology of rural Mexican women." *Health Care for Women International* 30: 614–628.

Wilson, R. 2007. "Acculturation and discrimination in the global market place: The case of Hispanics in the U.S." *Journal of International Consumer Marketing* 20(1): 67–78.

Worthington, R., A. Soth-McNett, and M. Moreno. 2007. "Multicultural counseling competencies research: A 20-year content analysis." *Journal of Counseling Psychology* 54(4): 351–361.

Zeichner, A., D. J. Parrott, and F. C. Frey. 2003. "Gender differences in laboratory aggression under response choice conditions." *Aggressive Behavior* 29(2): 95–106.

Zeitlin, J. F., and L. Thomas. 1992. "Spanish justice and the Indian cacique: Disjunctive political systems in sixteenth-century Tehuantepec." *Ethnohistory* 39(3): 285–315.

Zimmerman, M., and J. I. Mattia. 1999. "Psychiatric diagnosis in clinical practice: Is comorbidity being missed?" *Comprehensive Psychiatry* 40(3): 182–191.

Zimmerman, R. S., W. A. Vega, A. G. Gil, G. J. Warheit, E. Apospori, and F. Biafora. 1994. "Who is Hispanic? Definitions and their consequences." *American Journal of Public Health* 84(12): 1985–1987.

Zires, M. 1994. "Los mitos de la Virgen de Guadalupe. Su proceso de construcción y reinterpretación en el México pasado y contemporáneo. *Mexican Studies/ Estudios Mexicanos* 10(2): 281–313.

Index

About the Author and Series Editor

Author

MARIO A. TOVAR, PhD is a Licensed Clinical Psychologist, director of psychology services at the Rio Grande State Center, an inpatient psychiatric facility in South Texas, and the owner of Tovar Psychological Services, a private practice offering various services to the community. He has a broad background in both academics and mental health. As a faculty member, he has taught undergraduate and graduate courses in anthropology, psychology, and counseling and guidance at different colleges and universities. He is currently an Adjunct, Faculty of Counseling and Guidance, at the University of Texas, Rio Grande Valley. Tovar earned an MA degree in experimental psychology and a master of arts degree in interdisciplinary studies, with emphasis in anthropology, from the University of Texas–Pan American. He received his doctoral degree in clinical psychology from Walden University.

Tovar oversees the general functioning of the psychology department at the Rio Grande State Center, conducts psychological assessments and evaluations for a wide variety of purposes, and offers individual psychotherapy. In addition, he supervises an internship site for master's degree programs from different educational institutions. Tovar has given multiple presentations and training in his areas of specialization, and he is a Joint Commission Surveyor, a position that entails conducting evaluations of behavioral health facilities nationwide.

Series Editor

REGAN A. R. GURUNG, PhD is Ben J. and Joyce Rosenberg Professor of Human Development and Psychology at the University of Wisconsin, Green Bay. Born and raised in Bombay, India, Gurung received a BA in psychology at Carleton College (MN), and a masters and PhD in social and personality psychology at the University of Washington (WA). He spent three years at UCLA as a National Institute of Mental Health (NIMH) Research Fellow. He has received numerous local, state, and national grants for his health psychological and social psychological research on cultural differences in stress, social support, smoking cessation, body image, and impression formation. He has published articles in scholarly journals including *American Psychologist, Psychological Review*, and *Personality and Social Psychology Bulletin*, and *Teaching of Psychology*. Gurung authored a textbook, *Health Psychology: A Cultural Approach*, now in its third edition, relating culture, development, and health. He has made more than 100 presentations and given workshops nationally and internationally.

Gurung is a Fellow of the American Psychological Association, the Association for Psychological Science, and the Midwestern Psychological Association, and has served on the Div. 2 (Teaching of Psychology) Taskforce for Diversity, as Chair of the Div. 38 (Health Psychology) Education and Training Council, and as President of the Society for the Teaching of Psychology. He is also a dedicated teacher and has strong interests in enhancing faculty development and student understanding. He was Co-Director of the University of Wisconsin System Teaching Scholars Program, has been a UWGB Teaching Fellow, a UW System Teaching Scholar, and is winner of the CASE Wisconsin Professor of the Year, the UW System Regents Teaching Award, the UW-Green Bay Founder's Award for Excellence in Teaching, as well as the Founder's Award for Scholarship, UW Teaching-at-its-Best, Creative Teaching, and Featured Faculty Awards. He has strong interests in teaching and pedagogy and has organized statewide and national teaching conferences.